FOOTBALL'S SUPER
SPLIT
THE UNDERDOG DEFENSE

Bill Siler, MEd
Grant High School
Portland, Oregon

Leisure Press
Champaign, Illinois

Developmental Editor: Judy Patterson Wright, PhD
Production Director: Ernie Noa
Projects Manager: Lezli Harris
Copy Editor: Molly Bentsen
Assistant Editors: Christine Drews and JoAnne Hutchcraft Cline
Proofreader: Wendy Nelson
Typesetter: Sonnie Bowman
Text Design: Keith Blomberg
Text Layout: Denise Mueller
Cover Design: Jack Davis
Cover Photo: Ron Vesely/Focus West
Illustrations By: William R. Eckmann
Printed By: Braun-Brumfield

ISBN: 0-88011-301-4

Copyright © 1988 by Bill Siler

Library of Congress Cataloging-in-Publication Data

Siler, Bill, 1941-
  Football's super split.

  1. Football—Defense. 2. Football—Coaching.
I. Title.
GV951.18.S55 1988   796.332′2   87-22533
ISBN 0-88011-301-4

Printed in the United States of America

10 9 8 7 6 5 4 3 2 1

Leisure Press
A Division of Human Kinetics Publishers, Inc.
Box 5076, Champaign, IL 61820
1-800-342-5457
1-800-334-3665 (in Illinois)

To my wife JoAnne and our four children, Bret, Julie, Gina, and Jodie.

Acknowledgments

To the past players and assistant coaches, who through their uncommon courage, effort, and loyalty made my coaching experiences successful.

To coaches Joe Paterno, Jerry Sandusky, Jim Lambright, John Durham, and Bob Hitchcock, who gave me the ideas, fundamentals, and concepts through articles, clinics, observation, and discussion to develop, work with, and now write about the split-four defense.

Last, and definitely most important, to my family for standing behind me as I toured up and down the Pacific Coast in search of the ''perfect'' job.

Contents

Preface

When the subject of defensive football arises, coaches at all levels tend to declare a strong, almost defiant allegiance to the seven-man defensive front or its schematic counterpart, the eight-man defensive front. Their strong affinity for one defensive set as opposed to the other is matched by equally strong philosophical convictions about such areas as the use (or nonuse) of multiple defensive alignments, and whether an aggressive/attacking or reading/reacting defensive approach should be used.

Football's Super Split: The Underdog Defense was written as a comprehensive guide for coaches interested in knowing more about virtually any aspect of the multiple alignment/eight-man front defensive package. It is designed to be of interest to every head coach from junior high school through small college levels. Reasons to read this book will range from desiring to utilize the entire package to finding isolated ideas or just a better understanding of the defense so as to be able to coach against it more effectively.

The title is descriptive and should create interest in most football coaches. As "Super Split" suggests, we have taken the standard split-four defense and spruced it up with innovative alignments and schemes. Most coaches will relate to the *The Underdog Defense* subtitle because, frankly, most coaches are underdogs! The "underdog" label was not chosen frivolously. The strength of the multiple alignment defense (especially one with a split alignment as its base) is its ability to confuse the offense and make up for a lack of team size, strength, or ability within coaching schemes and plans. The defense that most coaches want to learn more about is the one they feel will help them win against physically superior teams.

Why Run the Split?

The split-four defensive set has been successfully run at high school and college levels for a number of years. This defensive scheme, an adjustment to the basic six-two and four-four alignments, has caused many headaches for offensive coaches. It is fundamentally sound, yet requires standard offensive blocking schemes to make special changes in rules to effectively block the formation.

The split alignment gained much of its popularity after successful use at schools such as Notre Dame University in the 1960s and Pennsylvania State University in the 1970s and 1980s. Many other college coaches have utilized the split scheme in their total defensive package. At the high school level, the system has been even more popular.

Since the mid-1960s, many additions and wrinkles have been made in the basic split concept. While some coaches have run the split scheme with a seven-man front (referring to it as the split-five), most coaches who adopt the split system do so with an eight-man front, three-deep setup.

This book provides a comprehensive manual that will enable you to develop a sound, variable split-four defensive system—a defense complete with your knowledge of personnel placement, techniques, adjustments, and drills that are necessary and compatible with the defensive design.

Throughout the book, you will encounter names and terms that we use with this defensive system. Some of these terms will be familiar football jargon. But others are unique lingo used by the coaches and players of our teams. These terms can be used with the adoption of the system. Old habits are hard to break, so I chose to use terminology familiar to me when writing this book. If you are content with your system's vocabulary, simply insert it into this system. There is no magic in the slang that we have chosen. On the other hand, there is a reason for giving each of the front-eight defenders a name. When working with multiple alignments and players who rotate to the strength of the offense, you will find it easier to refer to each position by a short, distinctive name. Also, when designing your schemes on paper or a chalkboard, you will not be confused by two Ss, two Ts, etc. If you have been calling your left defensive tackle, for example, just "left defensive tackle," you might consider giving him a unique name just for fun. High school ball players seem to like being called suggestive names. They may even play a little harder if they're referred to as Rambo, Butcher, Warrior, and so on. The nomenclature used throughout this book in describing the Super Split defensive system is listed below and shown in Diagrams *a* and *b*:

The Front Eight Positions
Strongside Defensive End = **SDE** = **Evil** = **E**
Weakside Defensive End = **WDE** = **Ace** = **A**
Strongside Defensive Tackle = **SDT** = **Rip** = **R**
Weakside Defensive Tackle = **WDT** = **Stud** = **S**
Strongside Outside Linebacker = **SOLB** = **Maco** = **M**
Weakside Outside Linebacker = **WOLB** = **Brutus** = **B**
Inside Linebacker = **ILB** = **Nasty** = **N**
Inside Roving Linebacker = **IRLB** = **Panther** = **P**

The Four-Down—The Linemen
Strongside Defensive End = **SDE** = **Evil** = **E**
Weakside Defensive End = **WDE** = **Ace** = **A**
Strongside Defensive Tackle = **SDT** = **Rip** = **R**
Weakside Defensive Tackle = **WDT** = **Stud** = **S**

The Linebackers
Strongside Outside Linebacker = **SOLB** = **Maco** = **M**
Weakside Outside Linebacker = **WOLB** = **Brutus** = **B**
Inside Linebacker = **ILB** = **Nasty** = **N**
Inside Roving Linebacker = **IRLB** = **Panther** = **P**

The Three-Deep—The Secondary

Left Cornerback = **LC** or **C**
Right Cornerback = **RC** or **C**
Safety = **S**

The Seven Spokes

The Three-Deep Positions = The Secondary (**LC, RC, S**)
The Linebackers (**SOLB, WOLB, ILB, IRLB**)

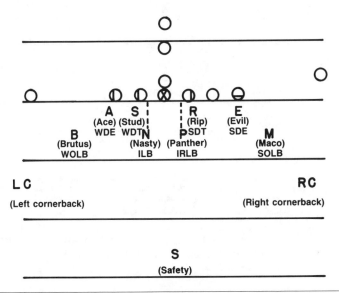

Diagram *a*   Super Split's initial alignment/coverage shown with a strong right call for "44 Omaha."

To facilitate your use of the defensive communications system, the offensive gaps have been designated by letters. Diagram *c*, designating those gaps, is printed here for reference throughout the book.

The "super" that this book puts into the split defense is a systematic approach to adding variety as well as spunk to the "generic" split defense. Like all standard defenses, the split alignment has inherent strengths and weaknesses. The spice that we add to the defense covers up some of those weaknesses, while adding even more to the strengths.

Almost every coach would agree that an underlying rule when adding anything to an offensive or defensive system is to not add so much that

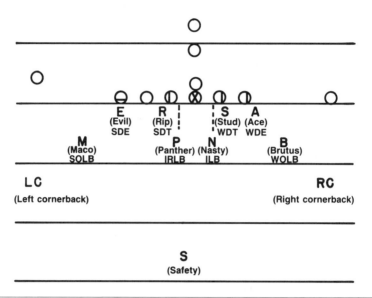

Diagram *b*   Super Split's initial alignment/coverage shown with a strong left call for "44 Omaha."

Diagram *c*   Illustration represents the offensive linemen from the center out to the tight ends. Each gap (space between the linemen) is identified by a letter.

you confuse the players. You want a sound defense, one that the players can play with "intelligent recklessness." The spice in this system can be added dash by dash to allow you to gauge the level of player comprehension as you progress to your desired level of sophistication.

Before describing the hows, whats, and whens of the Super Split defensive system, it is necessary to expose the whys for the adoption of this plan.

First, you can't make all of your decisions based on what is successful for somebody else. Many coaches have tried to copy major college or professional football systems. Usually these coaches soon realize that they do not have the time or personnel to make such systems work at the high school or small college level. The Super Split is a defensive system that, for many coaches, may be just what the doctor ordered. As when people are sick, if one remedy doesn't work, they may shop around until they find one that does. I hope you will find this system to be your remedy.

Second, the beauty of a variable defense is the ease with which you can adjust to the variety of formations, strengths, situations, and tendencies that your opponent will throw at you. Your opponent also will never really know how you will line up each week. Defensive surprises cause confusion, and the confusion leads to offensive breakdowns and dysfunction.

Third, the Super Split can be considered an underdog defense. It is a defense that can provide victories by confusing opponents and overloading blocking schemes. By and large, it gives you a tactical advantage that will assist you in outsmarting or outcoaching the bigger, stronger opponents on your schedule.

When confronted with a team that uses the split alignment, the opposing coaches must devote much of their practice time to dealing with changes that this unorthodox defense forces onto their blocking assignments. This burden on their practice time is intensified by the flexibility of the Super Split. Not only does the one defensive set (the split) present a problem, but the myriad of alignments requiring adjustments by their offense seriously overloads their allotted practice time. Your defensive game plan may only utilize two or three looks, but those may well be the alignments your opponent did not know about or did not have sufficient time to prepare for.

The ''bend, but do not break'' philosophy fits well with this defense. From the first day of practice, your *three-deep* (the safety and two cornerbacks) are injected with the fear of getting beat deep. By defensive design, their positions are segregated from the front-eight defenders. They will not be asked to rotate up and perform duties like those of the linebackers (as is often true of the four-deep secondary personnel). The secondary players will concentrate on the relatively passive responsibility of denying the long bomb, be it a run or a pass.

Accordingly, the front-eight concentrate on aggressively attacking the offensive running (and passing) game. The linebackers are not asked to rotate back to secondary positions, and the four defensive linemen are never asked to drop back and perform linebacker duties.

Because we don't switch assignments, what must be taught at each position is greatly reduced. This enables each player to hone in on his position and perfect the specific skills necessary for him to be a successful football player on a successful defense.

A last, but not least important, advantage of the split defense is that it is relatively rare and unconventional. The split is a maverick defense by anyone's criteria. Its uniqueness and reputation for creating problems for the offense puts an unsure, uncomfortable, almost negative feeling in the minds of opposing players and coaches. If opponents come into a game with subconscious negative feelings, your team starts the game with a mental bonus. You then must capitalize on your advantageous situation. By beginning the contest with aggressive defensive tactics and play, your team can make its opponents believe the worst of their fears. The vicious cycle has been started, and with the use of the Super Split, you and your team can keep it going.

Chapter 1

Who Plays Where?

The selection and proper placement of your personnel may be the most crucial decision your coaching staff has to make. Each group of defensive positions (the linemen, linebackers, and secondary) requires distinctly different athletic types to ensure satisfactory efficiency. The individual positions within each group also are differentiated and require certain qualities, while allowing for inevitable deficiencies. Size, speed, strength, agility, quickness, and coordination are some of the physical attributes (or deficiencies) that must be considered. Of course, intelligence, sometimes defined as "football sense," is also important. Physical and mental attributes coupled with what is probably the most important influence—a player's competitive attitude and inherent nature—must be evaluated thoroughly before making the final decisions of who plays where. Putting "a round peg in a square hole" can debilitate a defense and be disastrous for the individual.

Adding to this positioning puzzle may be the dilemma of having too many of a certain type of player. Many times you end up with an imbalance of players—for example, more linemen-type than linebacker-type athletes. We have found that to judge the player by his attitude and his quickness, as compared to other qualities, is about as accurate a deduction as can be made regarding an individual's second position. It is sometimes amazing what a great attitude coupled with the ability to get to the ball can overcome in the area of size and strength.

In most high schools you get whatever types of players come your way. Some schools with a sound "underneath" program can influence this situation, but usually your cards are dealt out of your immediate control. By keeping the basic responsibilities of the defensive groups (as well as the positions within each group) as simple and as limited as possible, you can reap the maximum skill of your athletes. The detail that you add to the defense can be the schemes that you devise, rather than an increase of skills and techniques to be learned.

Relative to the level of competition and to the available talent pool, a prototyped example of the athlete you are looking for at each position is reviewed in this chapter. The critical physical and mental attributes as well as each position's necessary competitive attitude and inherent nature are given. The bench press is used as an example of an athlete's overall body strength. You may assume his other lifts are comparable. Consider each athlete's total profile before making the final decisions of who plays where.

The Three-Deep

- There appears to be a strong correlation between good basketball-player types and good defensive backs.
- These positions require good speed, quick feet, timing, and good hands.
- Intelligence is a great plus, because scouting reports, films, and in-game tendencies and play actions can tip the observant secondary man and give him a valuable jump on the ensuing play.
- Mental discipline is a paramount virtue, since the rules the secondary players live by, e.g., "don't get beat deep," must override the strongest of instincts.
- Aggressiveness is a plus, but an overaggressive secondary man may get himself out of position.

Safety

You want your fastest, best jumper, and probably your all-around best athlete, at the *safety* position. The safety is very similar to the center fielder in baseball. An intelligent, extroverted leader as safety can be a real plus, because he makes most of the calls and coverage decisions for your secondary. Given the opportunity to select a stereotypical physical specimen for safety, a coach would look for a six-foot, 155-pound athlete who can run the forty-yard dash in 4.7 seconds and can bench press at least 175 pounds.

Cornerbacks

The *cornerbacks* may be designated *strong* and *weak* and also may be given descriptive names. With our system you would place the better of your two choices at the strong cornerback position. The cornerbacks can be a little more aggressive than the safety versus the running play. While a cornerback might not be quite the athlete that the safety is, he should still be among the team's quickest and smoothest. It would be nice if all secondary players were gifted athletes, but that is rarely true. However, if one is more gifted than the others he should definitely be the safety. When searching out likely cornerbacks, coaches should look for athletes about 5 feet 10 inches and 165 pounds, who run the forty-yard dash in 4.8 seconds and can bench press about 185 pounds.

The Linebackers

- The first thing to look for in a linebacker is an aggressive personality. This player should be physically tough and enjoy the physical contact of football.
- If you compare the secondary to a basketball type, you might compare the linebacker to a wrestler type.
- Linebackers need good overall body strength. Foot quickness is a necessity, although having "a nose for the ball" can overcome some deficiency.
- Football sense is a must to be a good linebacker. Some of this can be taught, but an individual's attitude and concern must be already present.
- The best linebackers truly love the game of football. They are frequently in the best shape of any of the players, and they make great conditioning captains.

Maco (Strongside Outside Linebacker—SOLB)

Maco should be a leader. He has to recognize offensive formations and situations and alert the rest of the team. He is the defensive player who calls out to the team which side to adjust their strength to. Speed is more important for Maco than for the inside linebacker, and strength may not be quite as crucial. A prototype Maco would be about 5 feet 9 inches and 175 pounds and able to cover forty yards in about 4.8 seconds. As strength is important to his success, he should be able to press at least 210 pounds on the bench.

Brutus (Weakside Outside Linebacker—WOLB)

This may be the spot for your fourth-best linebacker. Given the fact that a seven-man front defense doesn't even have a player at this position, it can be considered a bonus. Brutus should have qualifications similar to the cornerbacks'. He could well be your fourth-best defensive back on a team with more qualified secondary people than linebackers. He might even be your third-best defensive end, the type of person that you feel should start somewhere on your defensive unit. A typical Brutus would stand about 5 feet 7 inches, weigh 170 pounds, run the forty in 5.1 seconds, and bench press 180 pounds or more.

Nasty (Inside Linebacker—ILB)

Nasty, the linebacker who remains at the inside position on virtually all defensive calls, should be like his name—nasty! He should be the most aggressive, competitive person on your team. Many times he is the player that you build your defense around. His instant recognition of a play unfolding and his ability to react quickly set him apart from the average player. He needs the dedication to study opponents' films and scouting reports and to put forth 100 percent effort during the practice week. It is a plus if Nasty is a ''holler-guy,'' who also leads by example. Being without a formidable Nasty on defense is similar to lacking a good quarterback on offense: The prognosis for success is dim! For Nasty, a coach should look for an athlete about 5 feet 10 inches, 185 pounds, who can run the forty in 5 seconds flat or less. Nasty must be strong, so a 250-pound bench presser is almost a must.

Panther (Inside Roving Linebacker—IRLB)

This might be your third-best linebacker. Panther can benefit from a little more size and strength than the other linebackers because he is often asked to line up over offensive tackles. Discipline and alertness also will help him perform his assignments. He is generally not as free to just "play football" as is Nasty (ILB). Panther must adjust his alignments to various calls and game situations. Because he flip-flops from the right side to the left side of Nasty, he must remain composed during game situations and play under control. Although the typical Panther is a calm, cold-blooded tactician, certain teams' personnel change this scheme. In some situations Panther can be the extra linebacker who is set free to blitz, since you still have two outside linebackers and one inside linebacker. To successfully fill this position you need a player about 5 feet 11 inches and 190 pounds, who bench presses 240 pounds and can run the forty in at least 5 seconds.

The Four-Down

- Big, strong, quick defensive linemen are a welcome sight to any coach. A variable-alignment defense allows you the luxury of creating mismatches by aligning your bigger linemen over the opponent's smaller linemen.
- Because the involvement of your defensive linemen is more one-on-one, players who are strongly individualistic seem to relish these positions.
- Self-confidence is a plus, because a defensive lineman does not receive as much recognition as other positions (this is especially true at the high school level, where recognition for a sack is not as common because of the comparative lack of passing attacks).
- Some players have adequate confidence but a strong fear of failure. Because defensive linemen do much of their work hidden from the average spectator's view, players inhibited by visibility can still perform undaunted.

Evil (Strongside Defensive End—SDE)

The ideal Evil should be quick like a linebacker and big and strong like a lineman. Being kind of wild and unorthodox and having an aggressive nature seem to go with the position. Evil has to be good enough to line up and defeat the offensive tight end, who is typically one of the better big athletes on the opponent's roster. Superior quickness is a great weapon for Evil versus option teams and scrambling quarterbacks. Place your quickest defensive linemen at ends (Evil/Ace). A coach would like to get an athlete into Evil's position who is at least six feet tall and 190 to 200 pounds of muscle. If he can bench press 270 pounds and run the forty in 5 seconds or less, you've got a good candidate for Evil.

Ace (Weakside Defensive End—WDE)

This player need not be as big and strong as Evil, but ideally he is quicker. His personality is similar to Evil's, and he may even be a bit "crazier." If you are running a 50 defense now and are wondering where you will put your noseguard in this even defense, this is the place! In fact, as will be shown later, Ace is often moved inside to gap and nose positions within the confines of the variable Super-Split defense. The defensive end positions are probably the most fun on the defense. The adjustments and responsibilities are limited, allowing these players to simply "play football." A typical Ace would stand about 5 feet 10 inches, weigh 180 pounds and be very quick—at least 4.9 seconds for the forty. A smaller player could do the job, but you want a player who can bench press around 260 pounds.

Rip (Strongside Defensive Tackle—SDT)

Your best big man should be placed at this position. You will align Rip in the face of the offensive running strength. This may be to formation strength side, to tendency strength side, or to the side of the opponent's strongest blockers. Strength, agility, and football savvy are necessary for this position. Most of Rip's defensive reactions are based on movement of offensive blockers and backs. This "reading" technique is more difficult to perform than, for example, stunting or blitzing, so Rip should possess good natural athletic abilities. The fortunate coach will be able to line up a Rip with good height (6 feet 3 inches) and weight (220 pounds), with strength to match (300-pound bench press). If he can also run the forty in 5.3 seconds, it would be great.

Stud (Weakside Defensive Tackle—WDT)

If your weakside defensive tackle is not as big as Rip (SDT), he should be quicker. Stud will align on less formidable opponents than Rip and will be asked to slant or blitz more often. Often a coach finds himself with more defensive-end types than tackles. If this is your situation, you can readily move one of your larger defensive ends into this position. This second-best big guy (Stud) should be about 6 feet 2 inches, 210 pounds, and able to bench press around 290 pounds. If Stud is a little faster (5.2-second forty-yard dash) than Rip, it will come in very handy.

A point must be made concerning the use (or nonuse) of strongside and weakside defensive players. Many coaches believe that playing an athlete to only one side enables him to perfect his skills at that one position. They believe that having the athlete flip-flop negates any physical advantage the player may have because skills have to be doubled, thus reducing the time he has to work on them by half. This point of view is based on a logical assumption and has a lot of truth to it. If your two defensive tackles, for example, are more equal than different, you may choose not to move them from side to side. In a variable defense it is not required that you flip-flop your personnel to the opponent's strength. The assignments or responsibilities of the defensive call can be flip-flopped rather than the players. You may choose to flip-flop none or all eleven of the defensive players. When just the assignments are flipped, for example, the left defensive tackle may assume the role of Rip (SDT) on one play but Stud (WDT) on another. We have found it most necessary to flip-flop the linebackers. Once in a while we have had reason to flip a defensive tackle or end, but that has not been the norm.

Chapter 2

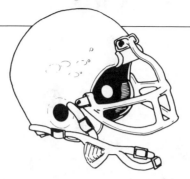

Defensive "ART" and the Four-Down Linemen

Defense is desire. This is a simplistic statement that most coaches would agree with, while understanding that it has many underlying qualifications. Big, strong, fast players make any coach look better, but they may be playing defense by chance rather than by design. The art, so to speak, of great defense is created by an individual coach's imagination combined with sound principles, fundamentals, and techniques. The acronym *ART* has been chosen to represent the fundamental components of sound defense consisting of the various *alignments/adjustments* (A), *responsibilities* (R), and *techniques* (T). The players understand that while the ART of defense is very important, it does not take the place of desire and great effort.

In the ART of this defensive system you give alignment assignments, which also indicate basic techniques and player responsibilities, by the numbers 1, 2, 3, and 4.

A #1 alignment is a gap position (see Diagram 2.1).

A #2 alignment is a position on the inside shoulder of an offensive lineman (see Diagram 2.2).

A #3 alignment is a position head-up on an offensive lineman (see Diagram 2.3).

Diagram 2.1 Rip (SDT) is aligned tight to the line of scrimmage between the offensive guard and tackle.

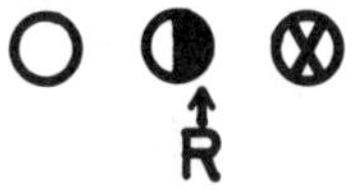

Diagram 2.2 Rip (SDT) is aligned on the inside shoulder of the offensive right guard.

Diagram 2.3 Rip (SDT) is positioned head-up with the offensive right tackle.

A #4 alignment is a position on the outside shoulder of an offensive lineman (see Diagram 2.4).

The alignment numbers combined with other terms and calls will signal your total defensive scheme, complete with alignments, responsibilities, techniques, stunts, and coverages. The numbers instruct the defensive tackles (Rip [SDT] and Stud [WDT]) where to line up, while indirectly

Diagram 2.4 Rip (SDT) is aligned in his basic position on the outside shoulder of the offensive tackle.

informing the remainder of the front-eight where to align, what to do, and how to do it. The first number of the two-digit combination tells the strongside defensive tackle (Rip) what position to take over which offensive lineman. The second number tells the weakside defensive tackle (Stud) where to line up. Unless told otherwise, the defensive tackles will always be aligning on the first man out from the center (the offensive guard). Examples of some basic calls are shown in Diagram 2.5.

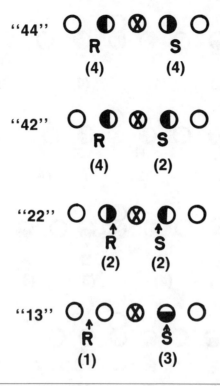

Diagram 2.5 Examples of some basic calls. Assume that the strength of the offense is toward the defense's left side in all of the diagrams unless it is stated otherwise.

Given no more information than the two-digit number (the defensive tackle's alignment numbers), the defensive ends will assume a #3 alignment over the offense's tight end or tight slotback. If there is not a tight end or tight slotback to his side, the defensive end will move down to a #4 alignment on the outside shoulder of the offensive tackle. Diagram 2.6 illustrates some of the four-down's basic alignment calls.

Defensive Linemen's Alignment Specifics

#1 Alignment

In a #1 alignment position the defensive lineman gets as tight to the line of scrimmage as possible. His stance, which splits the gap between the

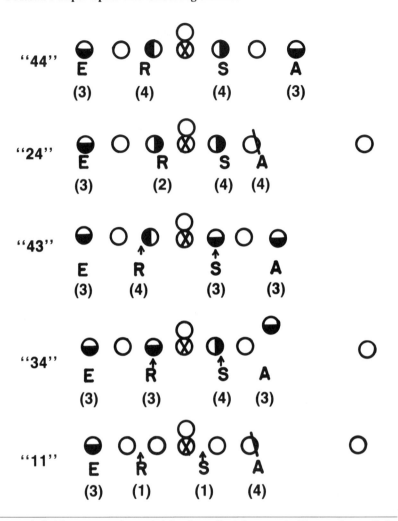

Diagram 2.6   Five commonly used defensive calls (alignments). The numbers tell the defensive tackles Rip (SDT) and Stud (WDT) exactly where to align. The defensive ends learn to automatically position themselves in a #3 alignment over an offensive tight end or tight slotback to their side. When facing a split end to their side, they slide down to a #4 position on the outside shoulder of the offensive tackle.

two offensive linemen, is adjusted so that the defensive player can get as low to the ground as possible and still be able to move quickly forward. This is best done by using a four-point stance, bending the elbows as much as 90°, with the chest about a foot off the ground. The player's legs must be up underneath him so he is able to extend and penetrate as far as possible into the opponent's backfield. By staying beneath the offensive blocker's shoulder pads, he will be able to split the blockers if they attempt to double-team him. This alignment requires that the defensive player react extremely quickly to offensive movement, exploding out of his stance and getting into the opponent's backfield. Your gap man should be coached to be aware of inside action, as he is very vulnerable to the trap block.

#2 Alignment

Your defensive lineman assumes a three-point stance, approximately one foot off the line of scrimmage, straddling the offensive lineman's inside foot. He should preferably have his outside hand on the ground and his outside foot staggered toe-to-heel with the inside foot. But you may find that a player does better maintaining one favorite stance for all four alignments—go with what works best for each player.

From the #2 alignment you would also prefer that the defensive lineman strike a defensive blow using the two-hand shiver technique (also referred to as the tripod technique). However, here too you might want to go with what works best for each individual. Some players will perform better using the flipper technique (described along with the tripod technique in the next section) regardless of their particular alignment. We make every effort to get the defensive lineman to use the tripod technique, especially in the #2 alignment, because it gives him a much better opportunity to work past the offensive blocker when the ball gets to the outside. Your defensive lineman in the #2 alignment is responsible for the gap he is lined up next to and for keeping his offensive blocker off of the inside linebackers. The #2 alignment is the most difficult to work from because the offensive lineman has positional leverage on the defensive lineman when the ball is being run outside. This necessitates extra practice time so that your defensive linemen can successfully execute their responsibilities. The #2 alignment is essential to the Super Split defensive schemes because of the alignment variety it creates and the problems it can present to offensive blocking schemes.

#3 Alignment

The #3 alignment is a head-up position, usually about two feet off the line of scrimmage. Your lineman will use his normal three-point stance. If both left-handed and right-handed stances are comfortable for your athlete, he should align with his outside hand down and his outside foot staggered.

The #3 alignment is used most often by the defensive ends over the opponent's tight ends and tight slotbacks. The defensive tackles are normally called to use the #3 alignment for more of a "bend, but don't break" type of setup. The tripod technique is, again, the technique of choice. If the flipper technique is employed, it must be delivered with the inside arm. The #3 alignment is the natural position from which to ask your defensive player to "read" the offensive blocker's head, to defeat the block, and to assist in covering both the inside and outside gaps.

#4 Alignment

The most common defensive tackle position is the #4 alignment. This position, which gives the defensive player outside leverage, provides the logic behind the use of the split alignment. The defensive tackle lines up approximately one foot off the line of scrimmage, straddling the outside leg of the offensive lineman. Using a three-point stance with his inside hand down and his inside foot staggered, he *keys* the opponent's helmet for his first reaction. Using either a tripod or flipper defensive blow, he attempts to defeat the blocker and maintain the all-important outside advantage. It is crucial when your defensive tackle is in a #4 alignment that the offensive tackle block down on him if the ball is to get outside. If the offensive guard is able to reach-block the defensive tackle, it allows the offensive tackle to block down on the inside linebacker, walling him off from his pursuit to the ball. If this is allowed to occur, your base defensive alignment (44) is seriously threatened, as shown in Diagram 2.7.

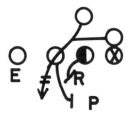

Diagram 2.7   A large hole is created if the defensive tackles allow the offensive guard to get an outside blocking position on them.

Your defensive tackles should work to perfect their #4 alignment techniques so that the offensive tackle has to block down on them when the offense runs the ball to the outside. Diagram 2.8 shows how this frees up the inside linebacker, at the same time creating a scrape-hole for him to get to the ball carrier.

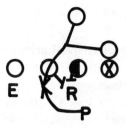

Diagram 2.8   The offensive tackle is concerned with Rip's (SDT) penetration and pursuit through his gap. When the offensive tackle is forced to block down on Rip, an excellent scrape lane is created for Panther's (IRLB) move to the ball.

It is very important that the defensive tackles do not get blocked to the inside by the offensive guards when in a #4 alignment, and the tackles' abilities are tested even further with inside trap play. The defensive tackles, while protecting their outside gap, must also have the necessary skill to shut down the inside trap play. The ability to successfully execute these two moves usually determines your starting defensive tackles and which one will be Rip (SDT) and which one Stud (WDT).

We have begun to add some spice to the basic split-four defense by creating a system of communication that allows you to routinely alter the defensive tackles' alignment from their basic position, the #4 alignment. As will be shown, the multiplicity of the defense is greatly increased when we add the various terms, calls, and coverages to the numbers.

Defensive Linemen's Responsibilities and Technique Specifics

You should keep the necessary *reads* and skills of your defensive linemen to a minimum. This will allow them time to refine the basic fundamentals that you determine are essential to good defensive play. Teaching the proper reactions to the various reads, skills, and techniques should be initiated from the base alignment, 44. You will recall that this alignment puts your defensive tackles on the outside shoulder of the offensive guards and your defensive ends head-up with the tight end or slotback. Your linemen ought to become proficient in their duties from the base alignment before moving on. Although the skills and reactions needed at each alignment are very similar, the feel for each position and its requirements is best obtained by concentrating practice on one position at a time.

Reading the "Hat"

The initial reaction of the defensive lineman is to the movement of the offensive lineman he is lined up over. This movement recognition is centered on the opponent's helmet, or *hat*. Your defensive linemen must learn to react quickly and decisively based on the movement of the opponent's hat. Although this is a learned response, witnessing a skilled defender reacting almost simultaneously with the movement of the offensive blocker would make you believe that it is a natural reflex.

Reactions to the "Hat"

Basically, the offensive lineman's hat can move in one of four directions. The hat may move forward, to the inside, or to the outside, or it may retreat (that is, move backward as when the offensive man is positioning himself to pass block). See Diagram 2.9.

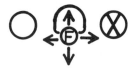

Diagram 2.9   The *hat* moves in four directions.

The "Hat" Moves Forward

When the hat moves toward him, the defensive lineman must instantly react and step to the blocker, delivering a defensive blow forceful enough to stop the blocker's forward momentum. Once the blocker has been stalemated, the defender must separate from him and move to the ball at the quickest angle. There are two defensive methods to defeat the offensive blocker—the *flipper* technique and the *shiver* or *tripod* technique. The choice of which technique to use depends on a number of player variables, such as size, strength, quickness, coordination, and experience. Most coaches would probably agree that a fairly gifted athlete should use the shiver or tripod method. The majority of college and professional players use this method of delivering a defensive blow by the heel of the hand.

Since the flipper technique requires less strength and coordination, you may choose this for your weaker athletes. The flipper technique falls short of the shiver method in the defender's ability to separate from the blocker. The flipper technique, delivered by the forearm, in effect handicaps the defender to being able to use only one arm when shedding off the blocker. It is in the area of strength required that the tripod technique proves difficult. An athlete needs extreme upper-body and arm strength to separate himself from a large blocker who is attempting to maintain contact. It also takes excellent coordination to extend or punch into the blocker at just the right time to negate his drive.

The Flipper Technique.   The flipper is nothing more than an arm bent at a right angle, with the hand facing down in a fist. Used with a short step with either leg while the opposite foot is planted, the blow is delivered up under the blocker's shoulder pads. This flipper must be delivered vertically, not sideways. In a #4 (or #3) alignment, when the inside arm is delivering the flipper blow, the outside hand is delivering a shiver to the blocker's outside shoulder pad. As the defensive blow is delivered, the defender's hips must explode forward, straightening the back and providing the punch in the defensive blow. As the offensive blocker's force is brought under control, the defender must extend his flipper arm and along with his shiver hand disconnect from the blocker.

The Tripod Technique.   With the tripod method, the defender takes a short step with either foot (in a #4 alignment you would probably prefer that he step first with the inside foot to avoid the outside leg being hooked by the blocker). The defensive lineman then delivers a blow with his hands and a "blow" with his eyes. The target for the defender's defensive blow is between and above the numbers on the blocker's jersey. This area, referred to as the landmark, is where the defender should "strike" first, with his eyes. If you emphasize to your players that they should initiate all their "hitting" with their eyes, they will be in the safest, most kinesthetically sound position possible. Using the term "eyes" will promote the desired results of a straight back and the head up. Most spinal cord or neck injuries in football are a result of a blocker, tackler, or runner dropping his head at the moment of contact. If you teach your players to "see" the hit, their heads will be up and their backs will be straight.

After your player's eyes "strike" the target area, his head will slide upward and to the side to enable him to see the offensive play unfolding. While his eyes are contacting their landmark, his hands are simultaneously striking the blocker in the armpit/shoulder area. The hands, with the arms kept to the inside, are extended forcefully along with the explosive forward movement of the hips. The contact with the defender's eyes will not be considered an illegal "butt," because the hands make contact at the same time and the head slides to one side or the other after contact. Because neck strength is so vital to the player's safety as well as to his ability to execute assignments, we have emphasized to the players the importance of having necks like bulls and putting their necks "in cement" when making a hit.

The Transfer Technique.   The *transfer* technique is used by the defensive lineman when the ball has gotten outside of him and the blocker has the outside position advantage (this can also happen when the ball is run away from the defender and the offensive blocker manages to get an inside position advantage).

If your player is aligned in a #2 or #3 position on the blocker and the ball moves outside of that position, he usually must perform the transfer technique to escape from his blocker to pursue the ball. The defensive man has to make every effort to stay in a square position (shoulders parallel to the line of scrimmage) and to keep the offensive blocker from getting too much of an outside advantage.

With either the flipper or tripod blows, the defender must control the blocker's outside shoulder with his outside hand. As the ball moves outside of the blocker, the defensive lineman will transfer his inside position to an outside position by pulling through with his outside hand (which was positioned in the blocker's armpit/shoulder pad area when the defender struck his defensive blow). As the outside hand is pulling the blocker to the inside, at the same time moving the defender past the blocker's face to the outside, the defender reaches up and over with his inside arm, with an inside-out "swim" movement. This transfer technique is a move of strength with the outside arm and agility with the inside arm.

It is essential that your defensive linemen can properly execute the transfer technique because of the many times the offensive blocker gains lateral advantage of the defender. The defensive ends must work especially hard on performing this technique. Because your defensive end's primary alignment is a #3 position on the tight end, he is very vulnerable to being hooked or blocked inside on wide running plays. Diagram 2.10 demonstrates a play where both defensive tackles and the onside defensive end might use the transfer technique to pursue toward the ball.

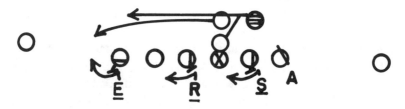

Diagram 2.10   Transfer action from a 24 alignment.

The Roll-Out Technique. When the defensive lineman has committed himself to inside penetration and is being blocked down on from the outside, he may be unable to square himself up with the blocker. In this situation he cannot use the transfer technique to get outside to the ball, and if he runs around the back side of the blocker, he will not be able to get to the runner. When your defender finds himself in this predicament, he must make a last-ditch effort to get back outside to the ball by using the *roll-out* technique (Diagram 2.11).

The defender, who has been temporarily defeated by the blocker, must quickly lower his center of gravity by lowering his hips, coming to an abrupt halt—almost sitting down on the spot—and getting his momentum moving backward and to the outside. Pivoting on his outside foot (the one closest to the man blocking him), he must throw his inside arm, elbow first, around behind his back. When performing this move he will jerk his head around along with his outside arm, looking for the outside escape route. This move is rather difficult and takes practice before a lineman uses it as a natural reaction when "walled off" by an offensive blocker.

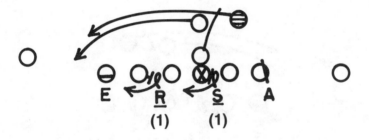

Diagram 2.11   Roll-out action from an 11 alignment.

The "Hat" Moves Outside

Your defensive tackles, when aligned in their 44 set, need to be especially concerned with the outside movement of the offensive guard's hat. They must understand that they cannot get hooked or reach-blocked. Versus hat movement to the outside, the defender takes a short, lateral step with his outside foot, thus maintaining the outside advantage. He delivers either a flipper or a tripod defensive blow, keeping the blocker off of his body and legs. The defensive player must remain low and square to the line of scrimmage when striking his blow. Here also, descriptive terms, such as staying "eyeball-to-eyeball" or "jaw-to-jaw" with the offensive blocker, help communicate to the defender the importance of staying low.

The defensive players also have to be aware that outside movement of the hat may signal that the lineman is pulling outside, which usually results in being blocked down on by the next offensive lineman to the outside. Versus this situation your defender will often have to use the transfer or roll-out technique on the blocker from the outside. If your defensive lineman has penetrated too far to be able to roll out, he will be forced to chase the ball from behind the line of scrimmage.

Another outside move your defensive tackles must watch for is the *influence* block. With this move the offensive blocker is attempting to sucker your defensive tackle to the outside so as to trap-block him from the inside. The defender who is being ''influenced'' should step first in the direction of the movement of the hat, then quickly determine the inside trapping action (which normally has a back diving into the inside gaps). Upon recognizing the inside trap, the defensive tackle must attempt to close the inside gap with lateral movement, staying low and square to the line of scrimmage. Diagrams 2.12a–d show the various reactions the defensive tackles may make when a blocker's hat moves to the outside.

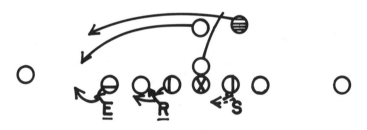

Diagram 2.12a   The defender's reaction to the reach or hook block is to maintain outside leverage and control his outside gap.

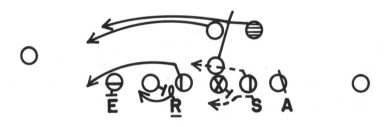

Diagram 2.12b   The offensive guard pulls outside and the tackle blocks down; the defender uses the roll-out technique.

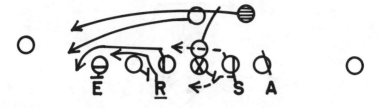

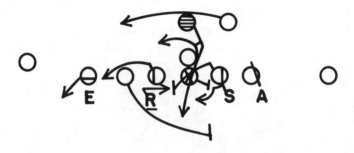

Diagram 2.12c   The offensive guard pulls outside and the tackle blocks down; the defender has penetrated too far, so he chases play from behind.

Diagram 2.12d   The offensive guard influence-blocks, and the play design attempts to trap the defensive tackle.

The "Hat" Moves Inside

The term *shut-down* very effectively describes the defensive man's reaction and responsibilities to the hat going inside. The defensive tackles are thinking "trap," and they react quickly by moving laterally to the inside, in a low position, square to the line of scrimmage. It is important that the defensive tackle get a piece of the offensive blocker who is going inside, to keep him off the inside linebackers. When meeting the inside trapper's block, the defender squats very low and attempts to defeat the block with his inside shoulder and flipper.

After contact is made the defender must *work across the face* of the trapper. To perform this move he uses the transfer technique and gives ground if necessary rather than going behind the trapper. If the trapper has done a good job and defeated your man, your defender uses the roll-out technique as a last resort to get to the ball carrier. The defender never wants to go around the back side of a trap block. Diagram 2.13a shows the defensive tackle shutting down the inside trap, transferring past the trapper's face. Diagram 2.13b illustrates the defender's attempt to use the roll-out move when the trapper has successfully executed his block.

Diagram 2.13a   Rip (SDT) first jams the man going inside, then works past the face of the trapper.

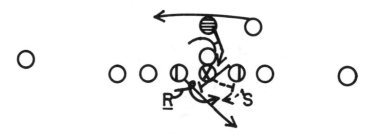

Diagram 2.13b   Rip (SDT) jams his man, then uses the roll-out move after being trapped.

The "Hat" Moves Backward

When the hat movement indicates that the offensive man is setting up to protect for a pass, the defensive linemen use only the tripod technique during the initial contact with the pass blocker. The defenders' first response is to close down the distance between them and the blocker. Using the tripod method, your lineman will stand the blocker up, attempting to drive him backward and get him off balance.

Pass blockers frequently get their momentum or weight leaning backward or forward, becoming off balance. The rusher must use the opponent's lack of balance to his advantage. When the blocker is off balance backward, the rusher should attempt to use his own momentum and strength to "run over" the blocker. When the blocker is overaggressive and leaning too far forward, the defender should pull the blocker past him as he moves to the passer.

The transfer technique will enable your lineman to rush either side of the blocker. The pass rushers must get in to the pass blocker quickly and should make initial contact with their eyes on the blocker's chest. The rusher's hands contact the blocker's armpit area, and using a strong pull with one hand while lifting the other arm over and in front of the pass blocker's helmet, your rusher will get in a parallel position on one side of the blocker. Once your defensive lineman has position to one side of the blocker, he accelerates to the passer.

The roll-out technique also can sometimes be used during the pass rush. One such situation would be when the quarterback moves out of the pocket, and the offensive lineman has outside position on your rusher. To continue to pursue the passer, the rusher would either rush around the back side of the blocker or would attempt to roll out underneath the blocker and pursue the passer from the front side.

Slants, Flips, and Penetrates

The techniques discussed thus far have been defensive moves that your four-down will use after reading the hat of the offensive blocker. With certain calls your defensive linemen will be asked to penetrate into an offensive gap as their first move. Although they will still attempt to read offensive blocking and backfield action, they will do so while aggressively attacking the ball.

Slants

Slants are predetermined initial-pursuit angles. When slanting, linemen should step first with the foot to the side of the slant. Since the purpose of the slant is to evade the block of the man the defender is lined up over, the defender wants to make himself as small a blocking target as possible. To do this he should drop the shoulder closest to the man he is slanting on while raising the opposite shoulder. This puts the slanter's shoulder pads vertical rather than parallel, reducing his opponent's blocking target.

As your defender performs his slant, he should be aware of the actions of both the man he is slanting around and the offensive man he is slanting toward. If he reads that the ball is being run in the direction of the slant, he accelerates to the ball. Your defender will get "in the hip pocket" of any offensive lineman who is pulling out to block for the runner and will pursue the play from the back side. If the slanter finds that he is moving away from the direction of the play, he must pull up and fight back to the ball. Many times in this situation he can use the roll-out technique. When your defender is slanting toward a man attempting to block him, he should make every effort to work across the blocker's face as he would versus a trap block. Diagrams 2.14a–c illustrate various situations the slanter will encounter.

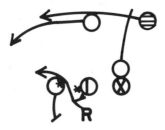

Diagram 2.14a   The slanter is beating the offensive guard's reach block and is pursuing to the ball. (Asterisks designate the portions of the offensive blockers that the slanter keys.)

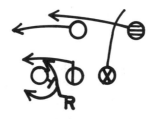

Diagram 2.14b   The guard is pulling, and the outside man is blocking down. Rip (SDT) attempts to pursue play in front of the tackle, but he may be forced to get in the guard's hip and pursue the play from the back side.

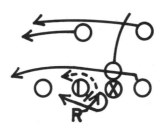

Diagram 2.14c   The defender is slanting away from play action and using the roll-out method to try to get back to the ball.

A slant involves all four defensive linemen. Slants may be called to the right, the left, the strong side, the weak side, or an offensive-tendency side. Normally the instruction to slant is called in the defensive huddle, but the direction of the slant is called at the line of scrimmage by Nasty (ILB). "Looks good" is the call for a slant to the left and "ready" for a slant to the right. The calls are usually repeated several times. Diagram 2.15 illustrates a slant left from the base 44 alignment.

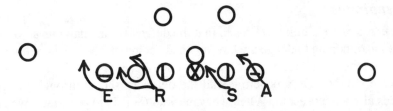

Diagram 2.15 Rip is slanting to the ball by penetrating the B gap or going around the down block of the tackle. The backside defensive end (Ace) jams the tackle and squeezes inside.

Flips

Flips are performed by the defensive tackles only when they are in a #1, #2, or #4 alignment. A flip means that your defensive tackles penetrate through the opposite gap that they are lined up next to. For example, if Rip (SDT) were aligned in a #4 position on the offensive guard, he would flip sides and penetrate into the backfield through the guard's inside gap. We use the offensive gap letters A, B, C, and D to tell the tackles which gap they are to hit. The techniques used to flip are similar to those used to slant. Diagram 2.16 shows the defensive tackle's flip calls from various alignments.

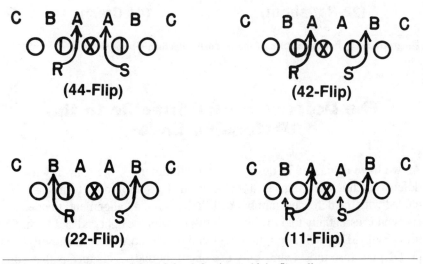

Diagram 2.16 Four examples of the defensive tackle's *flip* call.

Penetrates

Penetrates are similar to flips in that the defensive lineman hits an offensive gap, hoping to dodge the blockers and get into the backfield. Although the defensive ends may be called to penetrate, it is usually a defensive tackle's move. On a penetrate call the defender shoots through the gap he is aligned closest to. When we want Stud (WDT) to penetrate, we call "shoot." A call of "rat" sends Rip (SDT) on a penetrate, and "crash" sends the defensive ends through the C gap. To send both Rip and Stud on a penetrate, you call "rat-shoot." Diagram 2.17 shows the penetrate calls from various alignments.

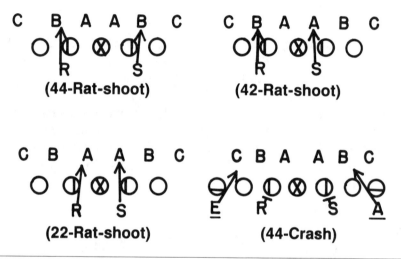

Diagram 2.17   Four examples of the defensive lineman's *penetrate* call.

The Defensive ART Specific to the Defensive Ends

As we have discussed in describing the alignment of the four-down, the defensive ends will align in a #3 position if no additional terms are included with the defensive number call. In his basic #3 alignment, the defensive end is essentially told to align jaw-to-jaw with the tight end and "whip" him (Evil [SDE] will align on a tight end much more often than will Ace [WDE] because most teams only use one tight end). This means that you want your defensive end to defeat the tight end's block, or his release off of the line of scrimmage, before doing anything else.

By defeating the tight end (or tight slotback), the defensive end will control the leverage on the flanks of the offensive formations. This is very important because it forces wide plays deeper than designed, which usually leads to their demise. Defeating the tight end also keeps him from blocking down on the inside linebackers and walling them off from outside pursuit. Another advantage is that the tight end cannot release directly or quickly off the line of scrimmage on his pass patterns or downfield blocking assignments. Handling the opponent's tight end is a tough assignment, but if you can control him it is a great bonus for the defense.

In a #3 alignment, the defensive ends almost always use the tripod technique. The stance of your defensive ends will vary among individuals. Some will perform better from a three-point stance, others from a two-point stance. Sometimes you will have the defensive end "squirm" his #3 alignment a little bit inside to help him keep the tight end off the inside linebackers.

The defensive ends are taught that any time the tight ends (or tight slotbacks) split out far enough for the defensive end to penetrate into the backfield without getting blocked from the outside, they should move down tight to the offensive tackle (#4 alignment) and penetrate.

The Defensive End's "Tight" Alignment

When the term *tight* is added to the defensive call, the defensive ends move into a tight #4 alignment on the outside shoulder of the offensive tackles. In this position their responsibility is to "lay their ears back" and penetrate into the backfield through the outside shoulder of the tackle. They do not have to worry about being trap-blocked from inside because their inside linebacker will fill the hole inside of them if the offense does succeed in trapping them out. Diagram 2.18 illustrates this situation.

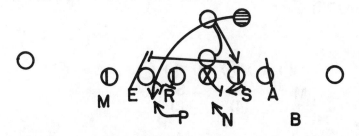

Diagram 2.18 The defensive end (Evil) is trapped, and the inside linebacker fills the hole. The defensive call is "Tight 44."

Because they do not have to worry about the trap, Evil (SDE) and Ace (WDE) may assume a very aggressive three-point stance, with a large inside-foot stagger. When aligned in the tight position, the defensive ends have four basic responsibilities, abbreviated as *PFCT*. PFCT translates into a statement of responsibilities instructing the defensive ends to *penetrate* into the opponent's backfield; to attempt to *force* the play inside (or deep if it is a sweep or option); to *contain* the ball or quarterback on drop-back passes; and if the play goes away, to *trail* it as deep as the deepest back looking for a reverse. (We adjust the trail portion of this assignment to a shallow path versus opponents that run a lot of inside counters.)

These basic responsibilities apply to the defensive ends in all outside alignments and adjustments. Of course, when in his base #3 alignment, the defensive end does not penetrate, but he does attempt to force, contain, and trail. Also, the alignment the defensive end assumes is very important to the success or failure of his assignments. A tight alignment, for example, makes it fairly difficult to force the play inside. Diagram 2.19 shows the defensive end's adjustment of his trailing responsibilities versus an inside-counter team.

Diagrams 2.20a–d display examples of defensive tight calls coupled with various defensive number calls. Notice how the inside linebackers adjust to compensate for the defensive linemen's alignments.

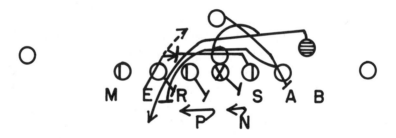

Diagram 2.19   Evil (SDE) is closing down inside rather than trailing deep. The defensive call is "Tight 44."

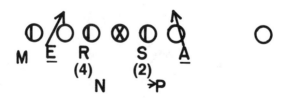

Diagram 2.20a   With a call of "Tight 42," Panther (IRLB) adjusts to the weakside B gap to compensate for Stud's (WDT) #2 alignment.

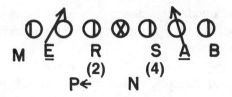

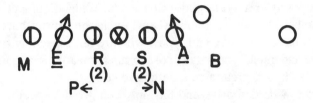

Diagram 2.20b   The call is "Tight 24"—Panther (IRLB) adjusts to the strongside B gap to compensate for Rip's (SDT) #2 alignment.

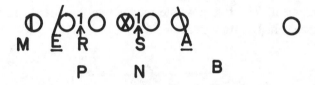

Diagram 2.20c   For a "Tight 22" call, both inside linebackers adjust to the B gap alignment.

Diagram 2.20d   With the call of "Tight 11 Stack," both inside linebackers stack on defensive tackles.

The Defensive End's "Wide" Alignment

The original split-six defense was designed with the defensive ends aligned outside of the offensive tight ends. The outside linebackers were positioned over the tight ends in a #3 alignment. This version of the split defense is very effective against teams with good outside running games. It is also an excellent defense to contain scrambling quarterbacks using sprint-outs and drop-back passing plays. The Super Split utilizes this alignment in an adjustment made with a *Wide* call. The defensive ends do just what the call suggests—they move three to four feet outside of the normal tight end alignment and crowd the line of scrimmage. They assume a crouched two-point stance, with the inside foot up and the outside foot back, and they look in at the ball for a movement key. The responsibilities of the defensive ends in a wide alignment are the same as when aligned tight—PFCT. Of course, now they are in a much better position to execute their containment assignment.

Many game-to-game adjustments can be made with the defensive ends in this position. For example, versus option teams, they are in an excellent position to go directly to the pitch man. Or you may choose to have them come down hard on the quarterback. Versus an outside-veer team the defensive end in a wide position could be instructed to break up the mesh between the quarterback and the dive-back. Against opponents who are predisposed to a Wide play offense, the Wide alignment is a great weapon to help you defeat their sweeps, pitch-outs, sprint-outs, options, etc. If you have defensive end types, who are not especially big but are aggressive and quick, you may choose to run from a Wide alignment most of the time. It is a great attack defensive set.

When the wide defensive end has not been given a specific game assignment, he keys the near halfback. There are five possible moves that the near-back can execute, and the defensive end must be coached to react properly to these reads. Your defensive ends use the near-back key in all outside alignments, but they are in the best position to use the key in the Wide alignment. The five possible moves that the near-back can make are illustrated in Diagram 2.21.

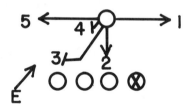

Diagram 2.21 Evil (SDE) keys the near-back, whose five possible moves are illustrated.

As the defensive end penetrates into the backfield, he adjusts his charge in response to the movement of the offensive back (who is aligned in the backfield) that he is closest to. Versus an "I" formation, he will key the first back that comes in his direction (if both "I" backs come toward the defensive end, he keys the front one). The actions and the defensive end's reactions are described here.

Action #1

If the near-back goes away, the defensive ends immediately think of the inside counter, quarterback bootleg, and reverse—in that order. Your defensive ends should develop the habit of informing each other when there is a slotback or wingback in a position to run a counter to the other's side. This eliminates the element of surprise, which usually makes or breaks the counter play. When the back goes away your defensive end should think systematically (as illustrated in Diagram 2.22): (a) Squeeze the counter inside by adjusting his charge angle down the back side of the line of scrimmage; (b) attack the quarterback's bootleg action as if he always has the ball; and (c) trail the play going away as deep as the deepest back, expecting the reverse or quarterback's reverse scramble action.

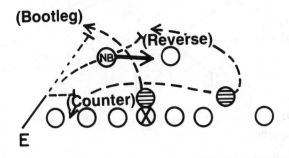

Diagram 2.22   The defensive end's possible responses to Action #1.

Action #2

If the nearest back dives straight ahead, the defensive end adjusts his charge angle as described for squeezing down the counter. He thinks off-tackle trap and dive option—in that order. Versus the off-tackle trap he again attempts to jam the play inside, taking on the trap blocker with a low, inside shoulder blow. In a dive option, the defensive end normally would have the assignment of colliding with the quarterback in the exchange area. In situations where you do not want the pitch man to get the ball early, your defensive end would be coached to string the option play out. This is accomplished by closing in laterally to the quarterback, but instead of tackling him immediately, the defensive end *skates* with the quarterback to delay his choice of keeping the ball or pitching it. If the quarterback decides to pitch, the defensive end accelerates at a proper angle to the ball. Diagrams 2.23a and 2.23b show the wide defensive end's reaction versus the near-back's dive action.

Action #3

When the near-back takes an inside-out approach to the defensive end, it indicates an off-tackle play. The defensive end must jam this play in-

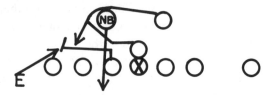

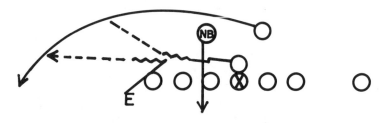

Diagram 2.23a   The defensive end responds by jamming the trapper on the off-tackle play initiated from near-back's Action #2.

Diagram 2.23b   In response to a dive option in Action #2, the defensive end strings out the quarterback with a skate technique.

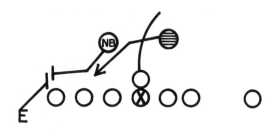

Diagram 2.24   Evil (SDE) keeps his shoulders parallel to the line of scrimmage, defeating the near-back's block with his inside shoulder and arm.

side, similar to the off-tackle trap play described for Action #2. Diagram 2.24 illustrates this action.

Action #4

A pass-block action by the near-back signals a drop-back pass or draw play. The defensive end is responsible to contain the ball, keeping the quarterback in the pocket. This is best done by rushing to the near-back's outside shoulder and attempting to defeat his block using the tripod method.

Many times the defensive end can drive the smaller back backward and can uncover the quarterback to make a sack.

Action #5

The near-back's lateral action toward the defensive end can sometimes be difficult to analyze—is it a sweep, a sprint-out pass, or a sprint option? If it is a sweep or sprint-out pass, and the near-back is responsible to block the defensive end, his angle of release along with that of the quarterback indicates to the defensive end which play is ensuing. Versus this situation the defensive end has to defeat the block of the near-back. According to the rules, backs are not supposed to cut block on outside running plays, but it still seems to happen often. To defeat these blocks, the defensive end assumes a low crouch, stays square with the field, and, using his inside shoulder and forearms, defeats the blocker. He must keep his outside leg free in order to come off the block and force the ball deep if it starts to get outside of him. Often the defensive ends have to shed more than one blocker. The skills necessary to defend against Action #5 must be practiced more often than those necessary for defending against any of the other actions.

If it appears that the near-back is releasing flat (parallel to the line of scrimmage), the defensive end will look to the quarterback. If the quarterback is releasing deep, it is a sweep or sprint-out, and your end would defend the play as previously described. If the quarterback is coming down the line of scrimmage, it is a sprint option. If the defensive end does not have a predetermined man to take on the option play, he utilizes the skate technique to string the play out. Diagrams 2.25a and 2.25b demonstrate the reactions of the defensive ends against both offensive attacks.

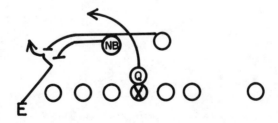

Diagram 2.25a   Evil (SDE) recoils off both blockers and maintains outside leverage (containment) on the roll-out quarterback. This shows the defensive reaction to the most threatening action versus an Action #5 release.

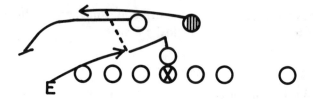

Diagram 2.25b The defensive end's predetermined assignment is to tackle the quarterback on the option.

Chapter 3

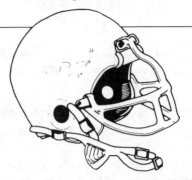

Coaching the "Heart of the Defense": The Linebackers

Intensity, desire, and aggressiveness are never more important attributes than when they are related to the success of your defensive linebackers. When your linebackers have practiced and mastered the "ART"-work of their positions, they will have the confidence and mind-set necessary to perform in an all-out, uninhibited, aggressive manner.

Linebackers' Alignment and Stance Specifics

As described in the section on defensive linemen, the alignment numbers specifically tell the defensive tackles where to line up and inclusively inform the defensive ends and linebackers where to position themselves. The linebackers' alignment rules are nothing more than a common sense adjustment to the defensive tackles' various alignments.

For example, when the defensive tackles are in a 44 set, both inside linebackers cover the inside A gaps, as shown in Diagram 3.1.

Diagram 3.1   In the basic "44" alignment call, the linebackers straddle the offensive guard's inside foot, while the defensive tackles straddle the offensive guard's outside foot.

When one or both of the A gaps are covered by the defensive tackle, one or both of the inside linebackers can align outside. This is illustrated in Diagrams 3.2a and 3.2b.

If the defensive tackles are in a #3 position, it is neither an outside nor an inside alignment, so the inside linebackers may assume a *stack* position directly behind their tackles. The stack adjustment is shown from a #13 set in Diagram 3.3.

Diagram 3.2a   In a 24 set Rip (SDT) covers the A gap, so Panther (IRLB) moves outside and lines up over the offensive tackle.

Diagram 3.2b   In a 22 set, both inside linebackers move outside.

Diagram 3.3   In a 13 set, Rip (SDT) is in a #1 alignment with Panther (IRLB) covering the inside gap, and Stud (WDT) is in a #3 alignment with Nasty (ILB) stacked behind.

Emphasize to your linebackers that they are first run stoppers, then pass stoppers. Texas A&M University refers to their linebackers as "runners," and we encourage our linebackers to relate to that image.

All four linebackers assume similar aggressive stances. We believe that opposing players make many subjective judgments concerning the toughness or "quality" of the football player they are lined up over. These judgments can be greatly influenced by what your players look like. This does not just mean how big they are or what color uniforms they wear. Rather, how a player carries himself, his football stance, and his body position project an image of the kind of football player he is. This subconscious judgment-by-association phenomenon can help or hurt your team depending on what your opponents perceive. Because of this, and to encourage our players to perform at their highest level of efficiency, we place "perfect" form as a high priority in teaching our fundamentals.

The linebacker's aggressive stance is two-point, with the outside foot staggered toe-to-heel with the inside foot. The feet are pointed straight ahead, shoulder-width apart, with the weight placed on the balls of the feet and the heels floating. The shoulders are over the knees, with the arms and elbows kept inside. The neck is flexed, and the back is straight. Asking the linebackers occasionally to reach down and touch the grass tends to keep them where you want them—jaw-to-jaw with the offensive linemen.

As already mentioned, your inside linebackers' positions are subject to the alignment that the defensive tackles have taken. Remember, Panther (IRLB) is the roving inside linebacker who does most of the adjustment to formations, field strength, defensive calls, motions, etc. Nasty (ILB) is the one to keep inside as much as possible.

In the base "44" call, the inside linebackers align about three yards off the ball, straddling the inside leg of the offensive guard. Panther (IRLB) aligns to the strong side and Nasty (ILB) to the weak side. When the inside linebackers are aligned over the offensive tackles (as in a "22" call) they align head-up, three yards off the ball. On calls such as "42" and "24," where one of the inside linebackers moves outside, Nasty stays inside and continues to straddle the inside leg of the guard. In the 42 set he has a little more leeway in his alignment, because Stud (WDT) is covering the weakside A gap. Diagrams 3.4a and 3.4b illustrate the movement of the two inside linebackers on the 42 and 24 sets.

Whenever the inside linebackers are stacked behind a defensive lineman, they have the option of moving up close to increase the chance of

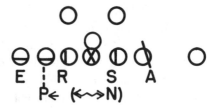

Diagram 3.4a **Diagram 3.4a** Nasty (ILB) stays inside on the "42" call and is able to roam from A gap to A gap.

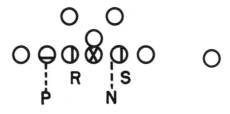

Diagram 3.4b On a "24" call, Nasty (ILB) remains inside to cover his A gap.

Diagram 3.5 A possible blitz from a 33 set.

a cross-charge blitz. This sometimes forces blocking changes for the offensive line. Diagram 3.5 shows this possibility.

The outside linebackers' fundamental alignments are not directly affected by the defensive tackles' positions. The basic alignment for the outside linebackers is three yards off the ball and three yards outside of the tight end. This alignment stays relatively the same to the offensive tackle's position when the tight end splits out. The outside linebackers' stance is very similar to the inside linebackers' (square to the line of scrimmage, outside foot back), except it may be a little "taller," as they are not over an offensive lineman and they must be able to look into the backfield. Diagram 3.6 shows the base 44 alignment of all four linebackers with proper foot placement.

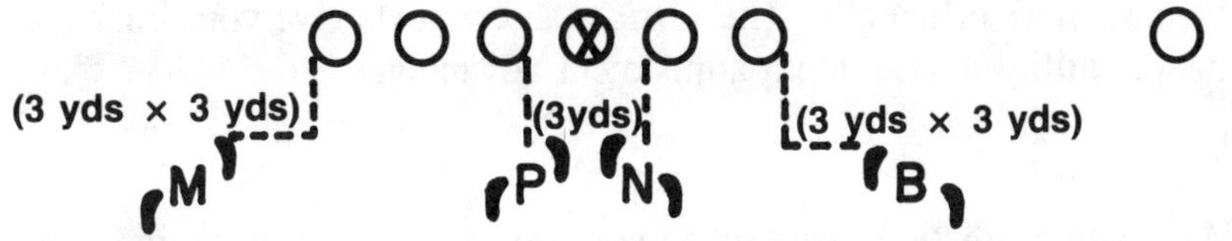

Diagram 3.6 The proper foot positions of the four linebackers when they are in their base 44 alignment.

These alignments are solely a starting point. Your outside linebackers (as will be shown) have a number of adjustments to compensate for offensive formations, personnel, and strengths.

Linebacker Adjustment Package

The standard adjustments that the Super Split linebackers make are initiated by defensive calls or by offensive alignments and game situations. The most basic adjustment is to offensive formation strength or to field strength (the wide side). Maco (SOLB) calls out "Maco right" or "Maco left," according to which side has the formation or field strength. The remaining defensive personnel adjust to the call, with Panther (IRLB) at the strongside-inside position, Nasty (ILB) at the weakside-inside spot, and Brutus (WOLB) positioning himself to the weakside-outside area.

The inside linebackers' most common adjustments have already been described along with the various numbered alignments that take them from over the offensive guards to over the offensive tackles. Both inside and outside linebackers often have to adjust how deep or how shallow they line up from the line of scrimmage. Sometimes this is a called adjustment; in other cases it is one the linebacker naturally makes to fulfill his responsibilities.

"Vertical" Adjustments

A linebacker's depth directly affects his ability to attack the line of scrimmage (to blitz), to pursue to the outside on wide runs and passes, or to drop back and perform pass coverage responsibilities. Shallow depth obviously enhances the linebacker's ability to attack straight ahead, while the deeper positions enable him to pursue wide plays and defend against the pass more efficiently. The *vertical* adjustments give your linebackers the versatility to use depth adjustment advantages.

"Up" Call

Many game situations arise when you want all your linebackers in an aggressive, attacking position. Short yardage, an all-out blitz, or faking an all-out blitz are examples. An *Up* call puts all of your linebackers approximately one yard off the line of scrimmage. Diagram 3.7 illustrates this adjustment.

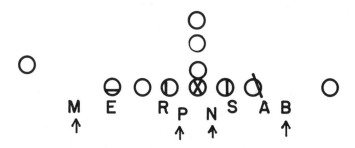

Diagram 3.7   The linebackers adjust to a "44 Up" call by lining up about a yard off the line of scrimmage.

"Back" Call

A *Back* call is considered the opposite of the "Up" call. When you expect a pass, or when you can afford to give the offense short yardage but want to be in better position to stop the longer gains, you can move all your linebackers back off the ball. The depth of the "Back" call varies with the situation, but a normal position is five to six yards deep. The linebackers also gain some width as their position gets deeper. Diagram 3.8 shows the alignment with all linebackers back.

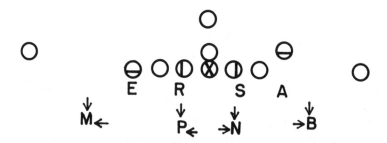

Diagram 3.8   The four linebackers adjust to a "44 Back" call by moving approximately five yards deep and slightly to the outside.

"In" Call

The *In* adjustment is a good defensive alignment to put the quick pressure possibility inside, with outside conservatism. While the inside linebackers are threatening inside gaps (possibly forcing blocking changes), the outside linebackers are in a good position to cover slant passes and outside plays. They are also in a better position to look into the backfield and pick up plays such as counters, reverses, and throwback passes. As will be shown, certain linebacker adjustments go hand-in-hand with certain pass coverage schemes. The "In" call corresponds to the *Mayday* pass coverage, which gives the outside flat zone to the outside linebackers. Diagram 3.9 illustrates a 44 "In" call.

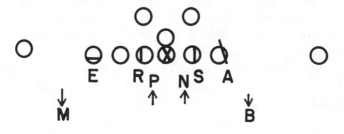

Diagram 3.9 All four linebackers respond to an "In" call, with the inside linebackers aligning close to the line of scrimmage in the A gaps while the outside linebackers gain width and depth.

"Out" Call

This linebacker adjustment coincides well with our base secondary coverage scheme, *Omaha*. This coverage has the outside cornerbacks covering the outside flats when the ball comes their way, which enables the outside linebackers to attack the play. The *Out* call puts your outside linebackers up on the line of scrimmage in an aggressive position, while the inside linebackers are back where they have great pursuit angles to the ball. In this alignment you may even give the responsibility of colliding with the wide receiver on sprint-out slant passes to the inside linebackers. The "Out" call is a good adjustment when you expect the offense to run outside of the tackle. It is a sound first-and-ten call. Diagram 3.10 illustrates the 44 Out set.

"Zigzag" Call

There are many situations when you want to attack on one side of the ball and play softer on the other side. This is often the case when the ball is on the hash mark. If you want your linebackers to adjust their depths for

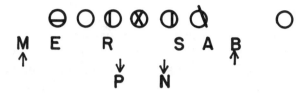

Diagram 3.10   In the 44 Out set, the outside linebackers stay close to the line of scrimmage, and the inside linebackers back off to five yard's depth.

this you can call *Zigzag*. This adjustment usually goes with the secondary coverage call (*Weak Mayday*), which has rotation to the ball if it goes one way but lays back if the ball goes to the other side. The Zigzag adjustment is called to the side of rotation. If your coverage is rotating to the left, for example, the Zigzag linebacker alignment would have the left side linebackers in an Out and the right side linebackers in an In position. Diagram 3.11 illustrates a "Zigzag Left" call from a 44 set.

Diagram 3.12 shows the defense in a Zigzag coverage call that rotates up to the right. If you use this adjustment often, players may come to call *Zig left* and *Zag right*.

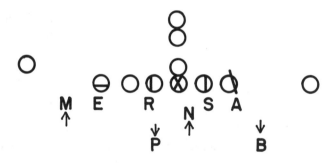

Diagram 3.11   A "Zigzag Left" call (or "Zig Left") from a 44 set.

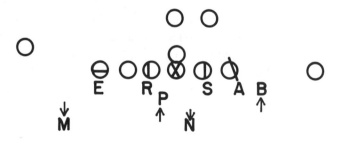

Diagram 3.12   A "Zigzag Right" call (or "Zig Right") from a 44 set.

"Slide" Call

There will be times when you want to move your linebackers as a unit to one side or the other. Often the offensive formation will dictate this move, but in some cases you just want more linebacker strength to an opponent's "tendency" side. The *Slide* call is often used to adjust to an offense's backfield man going in motion before the snap of the ball.

A call of "Slide" signals each linebacker to move one man over toward the direction of the slide. It also tells your defensive tackles that there is only one linebacker left inside to cover both A gaps. This instructs the backside defensive tackle to get into a position where he can help cover an A gap. If the tackle's initial alignment was a #4 position, for example, he would have to squirm over to at least a #3 lineup. Diagram 3.13 shows the normal "Slide" call, with the backside defensive tackle moving over to help cover the A gap.

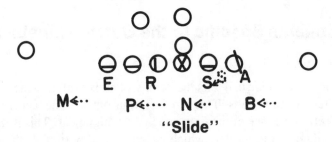

Diagram 3.13 From a 44 set, Nasty (ILB) sees the backfield strength and calls "Slide Left" to the defense.

A "Slide" call is automatically needed when the offense aligns in a *Trips* set (three receivers to one side). This could occur with offensive motion or with a shift. Diagram 3.14 illustrates the 44 set adjusting to a Trips alignment with the "Slide" call.

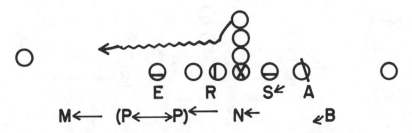

Diagram 3.14 Nasty (ILB) yells "Trips Left, Slide Left" to adjust to an offensive Trips alignment. Panther (IRLB) adjusts to the width of the Trips.

The Slide adjustment may be used with any defensive set. If, for example, you were in a tight 44 alignment, the adjustment would put Panther (IRLB) over the tight end and Maco (SOLB) would align outside in a walk-off position. Diagram 3.15 shows this scheme.

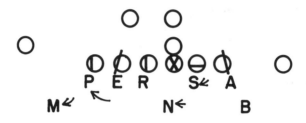

Diagram 3.15 A slide adjustment used in a "Tight 44" call: Panther (IRLB) aligns over the tight end and Maco (SOLB) aligns outside in a Walk-off position.

Adjustments Specific to the Outside Linebackers

"Wide" Call

Remember that a *Wide* call tells the defensive ends to align wide—outside of the offensive tight ends. This requires your outside linebacker to position himself in the face of the tight end in a #3 alignment. This is the most difficult alignment to master, which means a good portion of the outside linebacker's practice time should be spent in his wide adjustment position. Maco (SOLB) especially should spend more time in this position, because he will frequently be called to line up in a #3 position on the tight end. Diagram 3.16 demonstrates a "Wide 44 Out" call—a common Super Split set.

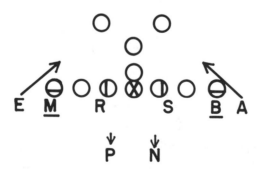

Diagram 3.16 A "Wide 44 Out" call: The outside linebackers are in the faces of the tight ends, and the defensive ends come hard to the ball from their wide alignment. The inside linebackers have moved back for better pursuit angles.

"Tight" Call

Here again, a call telling the defensive end where to adjust also informs the outside linebackers where to line up. Since the defensive ends move down in a #4 position on the offensive tackles, the outside linebackers must compensate and fill the vacant position left on the tight end. The outside linebacker does not align in a #3 position because the defensive end is in an outside shoulder alignment to his inside. The outside backer straddles the outside leg of the tight end in a #4 alignment and maintains outside-in leverage on all plays on his side. "Tight 44 Out," another common defensive alignment call, is shown in Diagram 3.17.

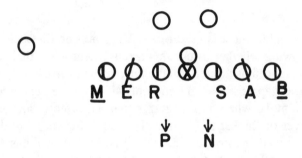

Diagram 3.17   A "Tight 44 Out" call: The outside linebackers are tight to the line of scrimmage, straddling the tight ends' outside feet. The defensive ends are inside on their tackles, and the inside linebackers are deep.

The "Walk-Off" Call

The *Walk-off* alignment puts the outside linebacker in a position about two or three yards wider and deeper than normal. It puts the linebacker in a position that takes away the slant or short post pattern of the wide-outs. It also gets him to the curl and flat areas much quicker. When the offense splits two wide receivers out to the same side, the Walk-off adjustment is an automatic response. Many times the "Walk-off" call is used to double-cover a wide receiver from the inside out.

The "Sniff" Call

When you want to harass and hold up the wide receiver's normal release off the line of scrimmage, you can do so and still keep deep coverage by putting your outside linebacker on the wide-out's outside shoulder. In a *Sniff* call the outside linebacker jams the wide receiver inside, covers the flats on pass plays, and takes the pitch man on the options. Diagram 3.18 shows Maco (SOLB) in a Walk-off position and Brutus (WOLB) in a Sniff alignment.

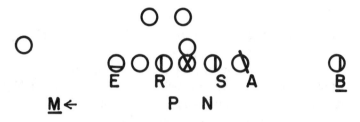

Diagram 3.18   The defense is aligned in a 44 set. The outside linebackers have gotten a pregame assignment to use the Walk-off adjustment to the strong side and the Sniff adjustment to the weak side.

The "Squeeze" Call

The *Squeeze* adjustment is used often. Your outside linebackers go into a game knowing whether to use this arrangement when their opponents use a particular offensive set. Usually the outside linebackers will squeeze down to the C gap versus a tight-end-only side. The defensive cornerback initiates the move when he recognizes that the offense does not have a wide receiver or flanker to his side. He yells "Squeeze" to the outside linebacker, who then moves inside; the cornerback then aligns in the position that the outside linebacker held. Often when this adjustment is used, Panther (IRLB) will be positioned over the offensive tackle. When this occurs on a "Squeeze" call the outside linebacker will instruct the inside linebacker to move into the B gap area. Generally, the linebackers are informed to line up over the gaps; specifically, the outside linebacker straddles the tight end's inside leg and Panther (IRLB) straddles the guard's outside leg. As you can see, this adjustment results in a split look over the offensive tackle's area. Diagrams 3.19a and 3.19b show the Squeeze adjustment both with the offensive tackle's area vacant and with it covered with the inside roving linebacker (Panther).

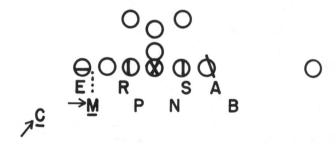

Diagram 3.19a   From a 44 set, the left cornerback calls "Squeeze" to Maco (SOLB), and they both move accordingly.

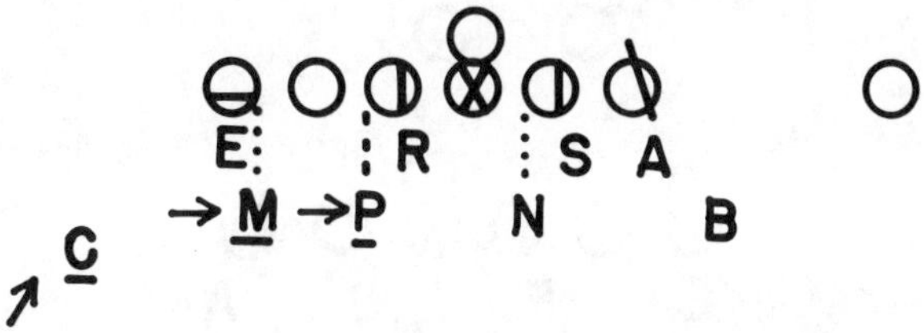

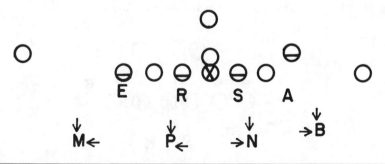

Diagram 3.19b This "Squeeze" call is made from a 24 set in which Panther (IRLB) is aligned over the offensive tackle. Panther moves inside to the B gap on the call as Maco (SOLB) squeezes down to the C gap.

Adjustments Specific to the Inside Linebackers

The only standard adjustment that affects just the inside linebacker is the *Stack* call. This adjustment becomes almost automatic in certain situations. When the defensive tackles align in a 33 set, the inside linebackers will stack close behind the tackles. This is a normal adjustment that may be made without a call. In the 11 set, where the defensive tackles align in their respective gaps, the inside linebacker will usually be told in each pregame plan whether to move to the stack position or not.

Selected Defensive Set-and-Adjustment Combinations

Diagrams 3.20a–i illustrate just a few of the more commonly used defensive set-and-adjustment combinations. Remember that a multiple alignment defense will only benefit your team when each player fully understands his basic responsibilities and the reasons that he is adjusting.

Diagram 3.20a 33 "Back"—a good long yardage set.

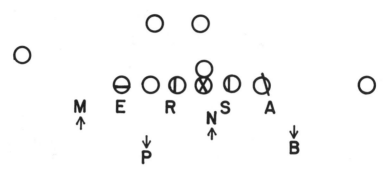

Diagram 3.20b 42 "Zigzag"—a good aggressive/conservative combination (zig left shown).

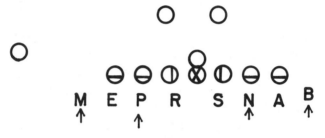

Diagram 3.20c 22 "Up"—an aggressive third-and-four look.

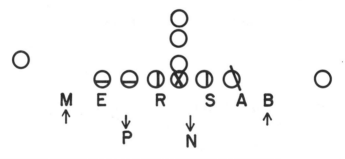

Diagram 3.20d 24 "Out"—a good attack-and-pursue alignment.

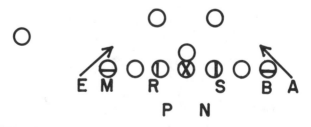

Diagram 3.20e Wide 44—a basic call for a hard-corner attack.

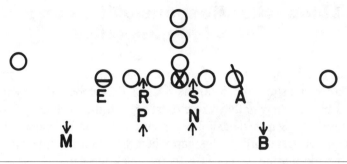

Diagram 3.20f 11 "Stack"-"In"—an aggressive-inside, soft-outside look.

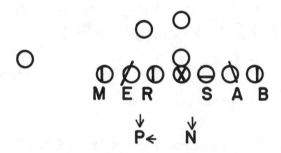

Diagram 3.20g Tight 43 "Out"—a strong off-tackle look with good inside linebacker pursuit.

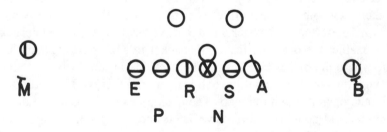

Diagram 3.20h 23 "Double-Sniff"—a good, obvious passing situation call.

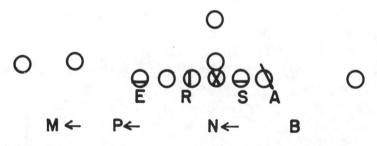

Diagram 3.20i 43 "Slide"—a normal adjustment to the offensive Trips look.

Linebacker Responsibilities and Technique Specifics

Diagram 3.21 shows which gaps your linebackers (and the defensive linemen) are responsible for from the 44 set. Remember, the linemen are responsible for the gap they are closest to, and the linebackers adjust to compensate for gap responsibility. Each front-eight defender should be taught to penetrate through his gap when the offensive lineman takes a split so wide that he cannot effectively block the gap.

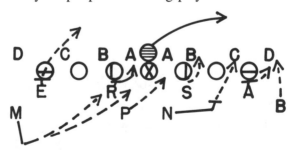

Diagram 3.21 The front-eight gap responsibility from the 44 set.

When the offense moves the ball laterally toward the left or right flank, the linebacker's gap responsibility is drastically altered. Whereas the defensive lineman delivers a blow and protects his gap and area before pursuing to the ball, the linebackers aggressively move to the ball, while being aware of their new gap responsibilities. On flow away, the backside A and B gaps are protected by the backside defensive tackle and outside linebacker. This enables the backside-inside linebacker to aggressively attack to the side where the ball is being run. The backside-inside linebacker attacks through the onside A gap if the ball is being run there or if there is a pursuit lane open through that gap. The onside-inside linebacker slides to a position head-up with the offensive tackle and protects the C gap. If there is a scrape-hole to the ball, he aggressively attacks it. Diagram 3.22 shows gap responsibility on peripheral rushing plays.

Diagram 3.22 The pursuit gap responsibilities (example shows ball moving to the defense's right) on peripheral rushing plays from the 44 set.

Reading the "Hat"

Like the defensive lineman, the linebacker's first read is of the lineman's hat that he is lined up over. Whereas the defensive lineman is close to the line of scrimmage and must defeat his man before moving to the ball, the linebacker is off the ball and able to see a bigger "picture." The offensive lineman's hat, along with the movement of certain other offensive players (to be shown), cues the linebacker's movement to the ball. Some coaches, for simplicity's sake, limit the linebacker reads to just one offensive man, whether a lineman or a back. This is a logical approach and may work better in certain situations. What your linebackers key on should depend on what you think they can successfully handle.

The "Hat" Moves Forward

Linebackers confront two basic types of run blocks—the *climb* (high) block and the *cut* (low) block. To be effective linebackers, your players must be proficient at warding off these blocks and getting to the ball. Versus a climb block the linebacker must step up and deliver a blow with an inside flipper underneath the blocker's shoulder pads. The punch of this flipper technique (described in chapter 2) is in the extension of the hips and the straightening of the back. The linebacker attempts to keep his outside free as he stays square to the line of scrimmage and disengages from the blocker. We have had some linebackers strong enough to use the tripod technique versus straight-ahead high blocks, but most players seem to do better with the flipper method. One problem sometimes encountered using the shiver method is that the player cannot keep his head up enough to see the play action unfolding. With the flipper action he can see the ball a lot better.

When the opponent comes out and tries to cut-block your linebacker, it is imperative that your linebacker be in a low, eyeball-to-eyeball position. He must use a two-hand shiver aimed at the blocker's hat and shoulder pads. If the linebacker is in a "tall" stance and is, in effect, delivering the blow on top of the blocker, he will actually be helping the blocker execute his block. For the shiver to have enough strength to stop the blocker in his tracks and allow the defender to escape, the blow must be delivered with the lower arm parallel (or near parallel) to the ground.

The "Hat" Moves Forward Shading the Inside or the Outside

Given this distance from the line of scrimmage, the linebacker can detect whether the blocker is attempting to run over him or to cut his lateral pursuit to the ball. The blockers may attempt to cut your linebackers off from pursuit with a low block or to wall them off from pursuit with a high block.

The first reaction of the linebacker to a lateral block is to shuffle laterally to a position half-a-man ahead of the blocker. Versus a climb block, the flipper technique is used, with the backside arm being the flipper. If the blocker is attempting to get into your linebacker's legs and cut him down, the defender shivers the helmet and shoulder pads, escaping to the ball. It is important that your linebacker, after defeating the block, stays half-a-man behind the ball carrier. His rule is to maintain a position half-a-man in front of the blocker and half-a-man behind the ball carrier as he pursues laterally down the line of scrimmage with shoulders square to the line. Diagram 3.23 illustrates the proper positions.

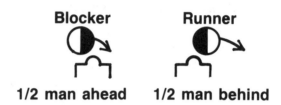

Blocker   **Runner**

1/2 man ahead   **1/2 man behind**

Diagram 3.23   The linebacker's desired lateral positions against an offensive blocker and the offensive ball carrier.

The "Hat" Pulls Inside or Outside

The linebacker's first reaction when his key pulls either inside or outside is to shuffle laterally in that direction. He must use his peripheral vision to pick up the action of surrounding linemen and backs as he determines the direction and type of play evolving. One of the linebacker's first concerns is that of outside offensive linemen blocking down on him and walling off his pursuit to the ball. Another important rule for a linebacker (especially the inside one) to learn is that it is better to give ground on a blocker who has position on him than to go underneath him and end up behind the ball. Diagram 3.24 illustrates this rule.

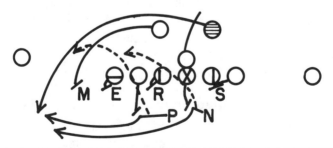

Diagram 3.24   A sweep play with the offensive tackle getting position on Panther (IRLB). the solid line gets him to the ball; the dotted line puts him behind the ball.

The "Hat" Moves Backward

A good linebacker always steps up on the snap of the ball, expecting or hoping for a run. When the linebackers read a pass, they have to shift to reverse very quickly and get back to their pass drop zones. As they retreat they read their *receiver keys* (explained in the section on pass coverage). Inside linebackers move laterally at first, then shuffle back to the hook area. The outside linebackers, when reading a pass, turn and run at a diagonal angle to the curl area.

Inside Linebacker Reads and Reactions Versus the Run

These inside linebacker assignments are described from the base 44 set. The reads and proper reactions are very similar from all of the possible alignments. The inside linebackers' total read includes the *triangle*. All of these reads will be shown, but remember that it may be better to limit the keys for the average high school linebacker. Once you do introduce him to the total key "package" though, he can work at his own pace to eventually be able to see the whole picture. You may need to frequently remind the linebacker that a key is merely a "hunch" to get started in the proper direction: He should not follow his key all over the field.

An inside linebacker reads the *near triangle*, which includes the lineman he is lined up over, the nearest back, and the center. If the quarterback does not reverse pivot, he may be included in the triangle. Diagram 3.25 illustrates the near triangle for both inside linebackers.

"Fast" and "Slow" Reads

Inside linebackers learn to react to their various keys with responses ranging from very fast to very slow or deliberate. *Fast reads* are set in action when

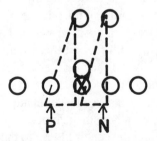

Diagram 3.25   The inside linebacker's line of vision and his awareness of the offensive center, the near-back, and the direction of the guard's initial movement.

all of the inside linebacker's key players in the triangle move in the same direction: All of them signaling one play. *Slow reads* are caused by key offensive players releasing in different directions. A fast read means that your inside linebacker can "lay his ears back" and fly to the ball. A slower read—more misdirection being presented—tells the linebacker to "stay home" and protect his area before sprinting off to where he anticipates the ball is going.

The inside linebackers are taught to work against the triangle versus certain basic running plays (in the drills, the linebackers work against just the backfield or just the interior linemen). The basic plays that the linebackers work against are presented from the fastest reads down to the slowest.

Diagram 3.26 shows the offense running a sprint option, which gives the inside linebacker about as fast a read as possible. With a read this fast, the linebackers can almost sprint (with good body position) to the direction of the key. Because their primary objective is to get to the ball, they must attempt to get past the potential blockers with at least a half-a-man advantage.

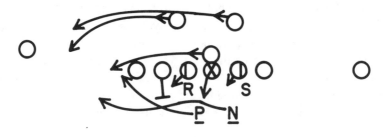

Diagram 3.26   The inside linebacker's fast read against the sprint option.

The dive or dive option gives the inside linebackers another fast read. But since the ball may come straight ahead or veer to the back side, the inside linebackers must be able to defeat straight-ahead blocks and protect interior gaps before sprinting to the outside. On dive action the inside linebackers have to shuffle to a position with a half-a-man advantage to the ball and to be set with both feet on the ground and shoulders square to the line of scrimmage when they deliver a blow on the blocker. Diagram 3.27 illustrates this.

Another play considered a fast read is an inside *isolation* play, designed to attack one linebacker, usually with the block of an offensive back. When "his" guard blocks out and the center blocks to the back side, the isolated linebacker must aggressively step up into the hole to meet the backfield

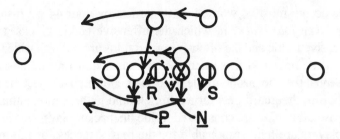

Diagram 3.27 The dive is considered a fast read, though not as fast as the sprint option action.

blocker. Your linebacker must create a stalemate before the blocker gets past the line of scrimmage. Because the back has more momentum on the play, the linebacker needs the better position. The linebacker has to have both feet on the ground and be in a solid, low stance when confronting the back's isolation block. The backside-inside linebacker has to fight past the head of the center. This is a play in which the running back may respond to defensive penetration at the point of attack by cutting back behind the center. The backside-inside linebacker must be aware of this and keep from creating a large hole to the back side of the center by looping around the center's head. He must aggressively attack the center's hat with a backside-arm flipper technique. Remember, the backside-outside linebacker has cut-back responsibilities and should be in position to help if the ball carrier cuts back behind the center. Diagram 3.28 shows the offense running an isolation play at the 44 set's inside gap. This is a play that can hurt the split look if not properly defended.

The off-tackle play is another fast-read play with cut-back capabilities. The various blocking schemes for the off-tackle play are numerous, but one

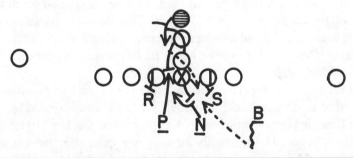

Diagram 3.28 The inside linebacker's reactions show the onside linebacker stuffing the blocker on the line of scrimmage and the backside linebacker jamming the center with a frontal position. The backside-outside linebacker is in position for the cut-back.

specific design must be worked on in earnest by your 44-set inside line-backers. The *fold block,* in which the offensive tackle blocks down on the defensive tackle and the offensive guard folds around his tackle to block on the inside linebacker, is often used versus a split-four defensive unit. It is essential that the onside-inside linebacker come up and meet the guard's block before the guard gets turned upfield and gathers momentum. This and the isolation play are considered inside linebacker plays—meaning that those players are held responsible for the play's success or failure. This is in contrast to the inside trap play (to be discussed under slow reads), in which the defensive tackles have the most influence on success or failure. Diagram 3.29 shows the offense utilizing the fold block on the onside- and offside-inside linebackers. Again, it is a fast read, but there is the strong possibility of a cut-back.

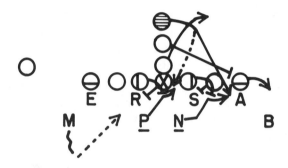

Diagram 3.29   The inside linebackers quickly and aggressively attack the folding guard, attempting to defeat his block before he can square up and block straight ahead.

Sometimes on action away from the inside linebacker, the center attempts to block the onside-inside linebacker using the *zone-block scoop* technique. When this occurs, a large pursuit hole, or lane, is created on fast-read plays for the backside-inside linebacker. This backside pursuit angle is referred to as *plugging* and may be a predetermined call versus some scouted opponents. Diagram 3.30 shows Nasty (ILB) pursuing an off-tackle play with a "Plug" call.

This seems an appropriate place to present an excellent offensive play designed to beat the split defensive set. The play was designed by a high school coaching opponent of mine, Len Lutero of Siuslaw High School, Florence, Oregon. Unfortunately for us, it was quite effective against our base 44 set. The play is intended to defeat the defensive tackle who is not doing a good job of shutting down the inside plays when the offensive guard releases inside. To make the play even more effective, Len lined

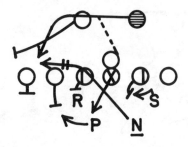

Diagram 3.30 As Nasty (ILB) escapes behind the center, he must go flat down the line of scrimmage, just behind the offensive blockers.

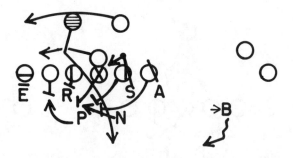

Diagram 3.31 Stud (WDT) aggressively attacks forward and puts himself out of position to tackle the halfback diving to the other side of the line. Nasty (ILB) has reacted so quickly to the fast read that the backside offensive linemen simply run him past the ball carrier's cut-back lane. Brutus (WOLB) is positioned too wide to be of immediate help.

up his offense in a wide-slot alignment that took our outside linebacker out of position to defend against the cut-back play. Diagram 3.31 demonstrates this play, which is nothing more than a dive–cut-back play with blocking adjusted specifically for the split defense.

To combat this play, Stud (WDT) would have to do an excellent job of defeating the offensive guard's hat as he shuts down with the inside release of the guard and moves to the ball. Nasty (ILB) can also be in better position up into the onside A gap. Being aware that an opponent might run this play and working against it in practice would be very advantageous. Diagram 3.32 illustrates the proper defensive pursuit angles to defeat the play.

A standard slow-read inside play that linebackers must work on is the cross-buck. This play is probably seen most often from the "I" formation. Often the tailback will jab-step to the side the fullback runs to, then hit the line to the opposite side of the center. Your inside linebackers should work against these typical cross-buck plays to learn to "stay home" and

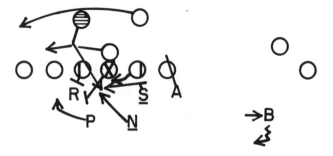

Diagram 3.32   Nasty (ILB) moves up into the A gap, and Stud (WDT) is in a lateral pursuit angle.

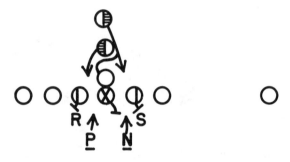

Diagram 3.33   The two inside linebackers attacking the A gaps. The farther they can penetrate up into the gaps, the less daylight the backs are able to run to.

protect their own gaps before trying to cover someone else's gap responsibility. Diagram 3.33 illustrates an inside linebacker defense of a simple cross-buck play.

There are numerous inside trap plays, but the one to be worked on most is the quick inside trap with the fullback. As mentioned previously, defeating this play is a primary responsibility for your defensive tackles. But the inside linebackers can't go running off with outside action and leave a big hole inside. The inside linebacker to the side of the trap has the most difficult assignment. He must key his guard's release inside and step up to help on the trap, but still be aware that the ball might move outside. He cannot penetrate so far up that the offensive tackle to his side can wall him off from outside pursuit. With trap action the backside-inside linebacker can aggressively attack the onside A gap where the trap is supposed to hit. Diagram 3.34a shows inside action versus the trap, and Diagram 3.34b shows why the onside-inside linebacker cannot afford to get walled off from outside pursuit.

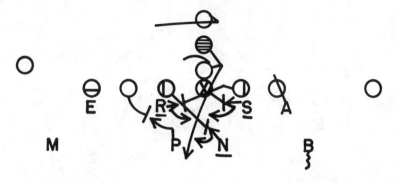

Diagram 3.34a The defensive tackles and the backside-inside linebackers do most of the work to stop the inside trap.

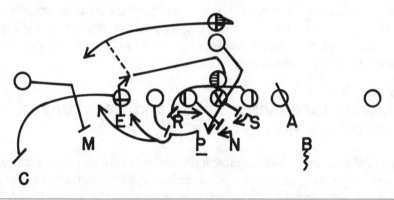

Diagram 3.34b The onside-inside linebacker remains in a good position to move to the outside if the offense runs the trap option rather than an inside trap.

It should be understood that these standard fast- and slow-read plays are substituted in place of your scouted opponents' specific plays. These base plays are used often in preseason practice and are intended to give the inside linebackers solid play recognition experience. You can't show your linebackers every play that they will encounter, but they can work intermittently on these common play actions throughout the season.

The inside counters and tackle traps are very good misdirection plays that come off of fast-read action. These plays, which hit in the inside gaps, are the defensive responsibility of the backside defensive tackle and the inside linebacker. If the counter hits wider than the A gap, it becomes the primary responsibility of the backside defensive end and the outside linebackers. Diagram 3.35 illustrates the defense of an inside counter. (The defense of the outside counter and the reverse are shown in the section

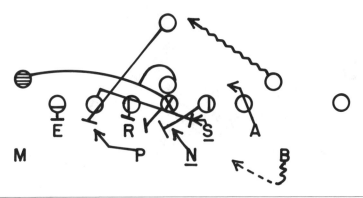

Diagram 3.35   Stud (WDT) and Nasty (ILB) shut down the tackle-trap, wingback counter.

on outside linebacker responsibilities.) An important coaching point is that whenever an offensive team has a wingback or slotback in position to run a counter, the backside linebackers should be made aware of them by a signal from the onside-outside linebacker.

Outside Linebacker Reads and Reactions Versus the Run

When aligned in his base alignment (three yards deep and three yards outside the tight end), the outside linebacker has keys and reactions very similar to those of the defensive end in his wide alignment. The outside linebacker must be aware of the tight end's block (or release) and the action of the near-back. When action is coming toward the outside linebacker (assuming he is in his base Omaha coverage rotation), his assignment is to attack the play and contain the ball. Before attacking the play he should check the near-back's release direction to determine if the play is hitting off-tackle or is sweep action. You do not want your outside linebacker to come up over the line of scrimmage versus onside plays that hit inside the tight end. If the near-back's release is an inside-out route (#3 action, shown in the defensive end alignment section), the outside linebacker must hold his ground to see if the play hits inside of the tight end or breaks outside. If the play is run inside, the outside backer can fill inside and make the tackle. If the ball carrier "bounces" outside, the linebacker can then come up and stop him. This action is shown in Diagram 3.36; you can see by the dotted lines that if the outside backer comes up to the outside too soon, he runs himself out of position to come back inside and make the tackle.

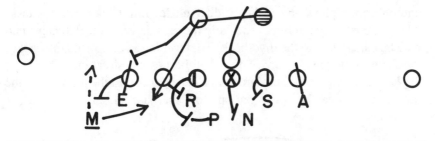

Diagram 3.36 An off-tackle play in which the tight end releases on Maco (SOLB) and the near-back kicks out the defensive end. The dotted lines indicate the outside linebacker coming up too fast and running himself out of the play.

Versus a #5 action release (direct outside attack) by the near-back, the outside linebacker checks the quarterback release. If the quarterback releases deep toward the onside flank, hands off, or pitches the ball to a deep back, the outside linebacker reads sweep action (roll-out, sprint-out, etc.) to his side. He immediately closes the ground between himself and the lead blocker; he wants to turn the play inside or force it to "belly" deep around him, ruining the play. The outside linebacker uses exactly the same technique as was described for the defensive ends. When attacking the lead blocker it is a necessary fundamental that the outside linebacker assume a hitting position square to the line of scrimmage, one yard underneath and one yard outside of the blocker. This position allows him to contain the ball inside, while not allowing the ball carrier to cut up inside of him or escape around the outside. Against an opponent with a strong sprint-out/roll-out attack, an "Out" call, putting your outside linebackers up on the line of scrimmage, can be very effective.

When the near-back with a #5 action and the quarterback release directly down the line of scrimmage, the outside linebacker reads sprint option. As mentioned in the defensive-end section, the outside defenders may have predetermined instructions to attack the pitch man or the quarterback on option plays. When not given specific game-plan instructions, the outside linebackers attack the quarterback's running lane in a low position with shoulders square to the line of scrimmage. As the quarterback approaches, the outside linebacker shuffles to the outside with him (using the skate technique described for the defensive ends), delaying the decision to pitch or not to pitch.

Outside linebackers learn this technique in their base alignment because it helps the defensive end with his responsibility of containing the quarterback on option plays. Sometimes the tight end blocks your defensive end on option plays and makes it difficult for him to perform his task. Also, against a dive option, especially the outside veer, the defensive end may be called to take the dive-back. So, teaching your outside linebacker the skate technique may prove quite helpful in some situations. Diagrams 3.37a–c demonstrate the standard option defenses against the inside veer, the outside veer, and the sprint option from the base 44 set.

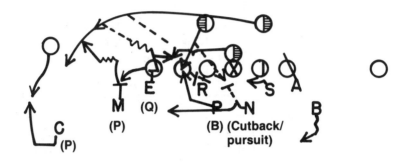

Diagram 3.37a   The standard defense against the inside veer: (P) = Pitch; (B) = Back; (Q) = Quarterback.

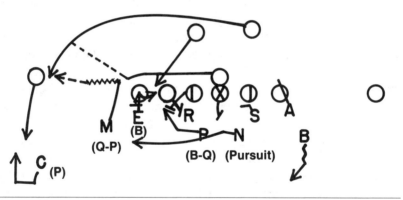

Diagram 3.37b   The 44 set's basic approach to stopping the outside veer.

There are numerous alignments and schemes that may attack a certain opponent's option series better than the base 44 set with the basic option rules. One example is the Wide 44 alignment against an outside-veer team or a sprint-option team. Also, against an opponent that runs all of its offense down the line of scrimmage, you may elect to go with a penetrating formation like 11 Stack or Tight 22. Option offenses like to run against basic alignments that they can recognize so the quarterback won't be confronted with new decisions or "looks." When playing a bigger, stronger op-

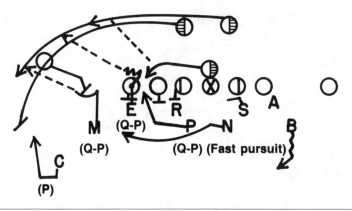

Diagram 3.37c   The 44 set against the sprint option using basic defensive assignments.

ponent that runs an option offense, your only chance may be to confuse them with defensive alignments and schemes. It beats accepting defeat.

When the ball goes away, outside linebackers have the big responsibility to defend against any misdirection play. Misdirection plays are not rare. Many teams at the high school level run up to 25 percent misdirection plays, which is an additional reason to use a balanced eight-man front. That backside linebacker really comes in handy versus inside counters, outside counters, reverses, bootlegs, throwback passes, drag passes, screens, etc. On the snap of the ball the outside linebackers step forward, anticipating a run to their side. As they recognize the initial play action moving away from their position, they begin to shuffle straight backward as they look into the ball. Emphasize to your outside linebackers that they will not make many tackles on plays that are run away from their side of the field and thus should not hurry too quickly to sprint laterally in the direction of the first play action. It will help them perform their duty if you teach them to expect a misdirection play that will return to their side. The outside linebackers shuffle back for five yards before getting into their pursuit angle to run down the play going to the far side. As they shuffle backward they systematically look for the misdirection play, from the fastest-hitting plays to those that take more time to unfold. They look for inside counter first, then outside counter. If it is a possible pass, they anticipate the quick throwback first, then look for bootlegs and drag patterns. The slower-forming plays, such as deep reverses and screens, are last in the order of concern. Diagrams 3.38a and b show the backside-outside linebacker protecting the inside gap on a quick counter and the outside gap on a slower outside counter.

As mentioned in the outside linebacker's alignment-adjustment section, his most difficult position to master is the #3 alignment on the tight end.

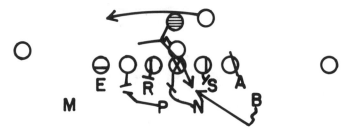

Diagram 3.38a   Brutus (WOLB) defends the backside A gap against the quick fullback counter. Stud (WDT) should also help on this play.

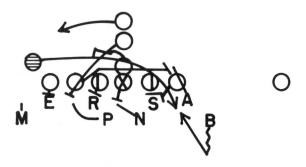

Diagram 3.38b   Brutus has shuffled back slightly deeper than he did with the quick-hitting inside counter. Although he has support responsibilities on the inside counters, his primary responsibilities are on the outside counters.

This is the position he assumes on a "Wide" call, and much of his practice time should be practiced from this alignment (assuming you use this adjustment frequently). The outside linebacker assumes the same responsibilities as in the defensive end's base #3 alignment, except for pass coverage assignments and the basic option scheme. When defending the option in a Wide alignment, the defensive end attacks the quarterback first, using the skate technique if not instructed otherwise, and the outside linebacker defeats the tight end and then has pitch responsibilities. Diagram 3.39 shows the outside linebacker jamming the tight end's release on the cornerback, and then pursuing inside-out to the pitch-back. The wide defensive end attacks the option quarterback and skates with him, delaying the pitch.

Linebacker Assignments Versus the Drop-Back Pass

This section discusses the linebacker's zone coverage responsibilities and techniques. "Man" coverage is discussed in the defensive secondary section

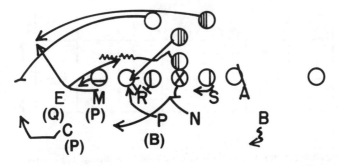

Diagram 3.39 The outside linebackers often have to pursue straight down the line of scrimmage to be able to reach the pitch-back. The two inside linebackers then must fill the inside A and C gaps.

on pass coverage variations. You may recall that the linebackers are coached to be run stoppers first, then to react to pass action plays. When the linebackers read pass via the offensive linemen's pass blocking and the quarterback's retreating with the football, they quickly retreat to their respective short zones as they key specific offensive receivers. The linebacker's areas of pass coverage responsibility are broken up into seven short zones. The zones' vertical depth reaches a maximum of fifteen yards. Versus opponents that run very short routes, the linebackers need only be responsible for patterns run under ten to twelve yards. The seven horizontal zones tend to become wider or narrower depending on the offensive field position or formation variation. In typical situations the *hook* area is directly in front of the tight end's position, the *curl* area is just inside the wide receiver's position, and the *flat* area is outside of the widest receiver's position. The middle area—between the two hook zones—is referred to as "no-man's land." The inside linebackers are instructed not to let receivers into this area without abundant harassment. There are times when a particular zone will be, in essence, nonexistent. For example, if the offensive formation does not have a wide receiver to one side, the defense does not have a curl zone to cover. It is important for your linebackers to have a solid understanding of the zones to be covered and when to cover them. Diagram 3.40 illustrates the seven fundamental "underneath" pass route zones. Each zone, without adjustment to formation or ball placement, is approximately seven yards wide. For purposes of communication, the offense's eligible receivers (quarterback not included) are numbered from the strong side (the side that Maco [SOLB] aligns to) across the formation to the weak side. Diagram 3.41 shows the numbers assigned to the offensive receivers when Maco aligns to the left.

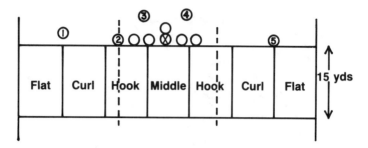

Diagram 3.40 Seven separate short passing zones, identified and labeled in horizontal areas that reach up to fifteen yards in vertical depth.

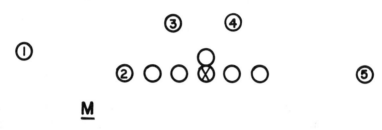

Diagram 3.41 Designation of the offensive receivers: strongside flanker, #1; tight end, #2; fullback, #3; tailback, #4; and weakside split end, #5.

Diagram 3.42 shows the receivers' numbers when Maco (SOLB) is aligned to the right and the offense is running from an "I" formation.

When aligned against a standard pro set (two wide receivers and a tight end), both outside linebackers key the movement of the second receiver from the outside. For Maco (SOLB) this would be the #2 receiver (the tight end), and for Brutus (WOLB) the #4 receiver (the near-back). As pass action shows, the outside linebackers sprint back at a 45° angle to

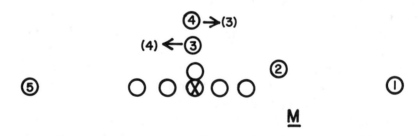

Diagram 3.42 In the "I" formation, the fullback is designated as the #3 receiver and the tailback as #4. These assignments would reverse immediately if on the snap of the ball that fullback were to move to the weak side and the tailback to the strong side.

a position twelve to fifteen yards deep and three yards inside the outside receiver's position. You do not want them to shuffle back because they cannot retreat quickly enough by shuffling to get the desired depth and width in the time available. You want them to drop the outside foot while continuing to read their keys (including the action of the player with the ball) and to run to their coverage zone. When the quarterback sets up to pass, the linebackers break down in a squared-up football position, ready to defend against the pass. The outside linebackers should be coached to always check the distance of the outside receiver's split before the snap of the ball. That way they will have a good "mind's-eye" view of where the curl area is located when responding to a drop-back pass. As was stated, the outside linebackers are keying either the #2 or the #4 receiver as they retreat. This does not mean that they are looking right at those receivers. The backers' eyes are focused on the man with the ball—the quarterback; they see their receivers' movements with peripheral vision.

The outside linebacker learns to react to his key receiver's release systematically. The first "second receiver in" release (or nonrelease) your linebackers are taught to respond to is when the receivers either set up to pass block or release on an inside pass route. When this action occurs, the outside linebacker realizes that he is released from inside pass coverage duty and may focus all his effort on defending against the wide receiver's route. As previously explained, he sprints to the curl area first; then, by reading the quarterback's eyes (we teach our linebackers to focus on the quarterback's pupils to actually see the expression on his face which will give them a jump on the ball as it is being thrown), he will work to the area the quarterback is looking to. The cornerback to the side of the outside linebacker may call out the wide receiver's short route. If the wide receiver is running a curl pattern, the cornerback yells to his outside linebacker, "Curl—curl"; if a flat route, he would yell, "Flat—flat." This, of course, is a big help to your outside linebackers because the wide receivers are behind them and consequently out of view. Diagram 3.43 illustrates the #2 receiver running an inside hook route and the near-back (the #4 receiver) pass-blocking. Both outside linebackers are free to "lock on" to the wide receiver's short route.

The second fundamental pattern that the outside linebackers work against is the short outside release of the second receiver in. This may be a *flare* route or a flat route. When the #2 or #4 receivers cross the face of the outside linebackers, the backers will release from their curl position and cover the flat area. Diagram 3.44 shows the #2 receiver running a flat route and the #4 receiver running a flare route. Both outside linebackers work to the curl area first, then break to the flat area to cover their key's

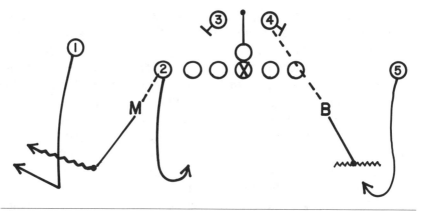

Diagram 3.43 Maco (SOLB) defends against the wide receiver's flat pattern, and Brutus (WOLB) protects against his wide receiver's curl pattern.

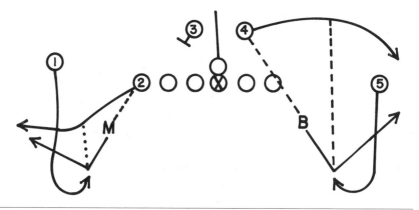

Diagram 3.44 The outside linebackers defend against common two-receiver patterns. The most threatening of the two, the inside pattern, is covered first.

pattern. It must be emphasized again that the linebackers are to focus on the quarterback's eyes—they do not break to these areas until the quarterback looks to their side of the field.

The inside linebackers have a more difficult read on drop-back passes than do the outside linebackers. Both inside linebackers have to read the release of more than one receiver. During drop-back pass action, the inside linebackers first key the #3 receiver to determine the direction the backs are moving and to be made aware of flood patterns. The inside linebackers retreat to their pass coverage zones by shuffling backward while keeping their shoulders square to the line of scrimmage. They do not turn and run like the outside linebackers do; they do not have as far to go, they have more reads to make, and they must be in position to quickly adjust lateral or vertical movement. When the #3 receiver shows pass block, the inside linebackers shift their key to the second receiver in from their side. In a base alignment, Panther (IRLB) would quickly pick up the action of the tight end (#2 receiver), and Nasty (ILB) would be aware of the remaining back's release (#4 receiver). When the #2 and #4 receivers release on an inside route, the inside linebackers get themselves in a good inside-out position and deny the receivers access to the middle zone area. If the receivers attempt to run a pattern over the middle, the backers knock them down or at least severely disrupt the pattern's path and timing. The inside linebackers retreat with their receivers' inside route and lock on to them from underneath if the receivers pull up in the hook area. From this position the linebackers cover their receivers' efforts to get open in the inside zone areas. Diagram 3.45 demonstrates all four linebackers defending against the drop-back pass when the #2 and #4 receivers release on an inside route.

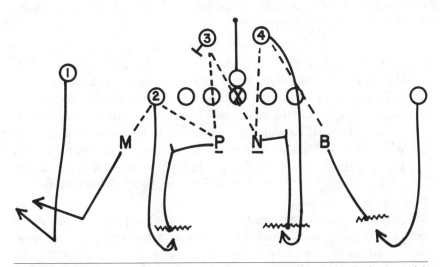

Diagram 3.45 Four receivers running short-zone patterns. The inside linebackers pick up the inside patterns; the outside linebackers read their keys and pick up the widest patterns.

When the #2 or #4 inside receivers run the short outside routes versus all four linebackers, their wide release enables the inside linebackers to move to the outside and defend against the wide receiver's curl pattern. The outside linebackers are also reacting to the inside receiver's release (as previously described) and move to cover the outside flat area as the receiver crosses their face. This pattern is worked against often because

it is standard in almost every opponent's playbook. Practice repetition greatly improves the linebackers' ability to exchange coverage areas as they
read the pass routes. Diagram 3.46 demonstrates the inside linebacker being
taken to the outside with the inside receiver's outside release while the
outside backers are "bumped" to the flats.

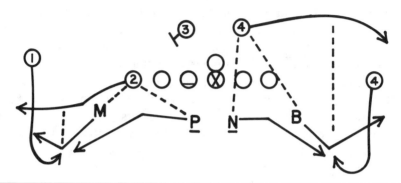

Diagram 3.46   To successfully defend against the wider patterns, all four linebackers
work together by reading individual keys.

To complicate matters, the #3 receiver may release into the pattern. If
he releases to the strong side, that would normally put three receivers to
that side, creating a strongside *flood* pattern. Remember that both inside
linebackers first look to the #3 receiver as they begin to retreat and cover
their areas. Nasty (ILB) will yell "Flood" in this situation and move to
the strong side. His assignment versus strong flood action is to pick up
any inside receiver releasing to the inside, keeping him out of the middle
area and covering the strongside hook zone. If the #2 receiver were running a *drag* pattern across the formation, Nasty (ILB) would pick him up
and cover him man-to-man. Panther (IRLB) will react to the #3 receiver's
release and the "Flood" call from his inside linebacker position by moving quickly out to cover the curl area. A strongside flood pattern will result
in your defensive linebackers moving to a position to cover all three of
the strongside short zones. Your backside-outside linebacker is left with
the responsibility of covering his wide receiver's short pattern. He will
lock on to him man-to-man versus short patterns if the #4 receiver does
not release on a pass. Diagrams 3.47 a, b, and c show the four linebackers
defending against three common flood patterns.

A weakside flood pattern is very similar to the strongside pattern, except the linebacker coverage assignments are switched. Nasty (ILB) still
makes the "Flood" call as he sees the #3 receiver release to the weak

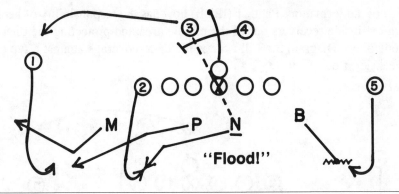

Diagram 3.47a   The #3 receiver runs a flare pattern to open up the curl and hook patterns.

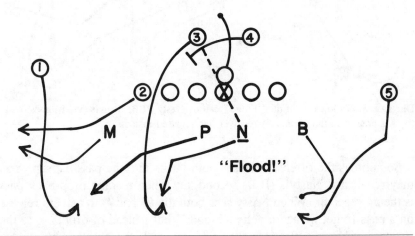

Diagram 3.47b   Similar to a flare pattern, a flood pattern has the tight end sprinting to the flats and the #3 receiver coming inside.

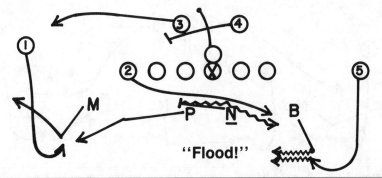

Diagram 3.47c   On this pattern, flood action was shown, but the tight end is dragging across the formation. Nasty (ILB) must be aware of this and pick him up.

side of the formation. Panther (IRLB) now has the responsibility of keeping the inside receivers out of the middle area and protecting the onside hook zone. Diagram 3.48 illustrates the undercoverage against a typical weakside flood play.

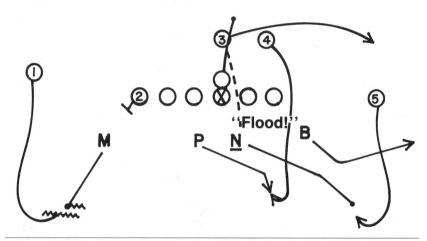

Diagram 3.48   Because of the "Flood" call by Nasty (ILB), Brutus (WLB) goes out to the flat area even though his #4 receiver has released inside.

Sometimes the offense releases both backs into the pass pattern. You may recall that Nasty's (ILB) second key when reading drop-back pass is the #4 receiver. When Nasty sees both the #3 and #4 receivers release on a pass route, he again yells "Flood," but instead of dropping to the strong side, he shuffles straight back and reads the quarterback's eyes. If the quarterback "looks strong," Nasty covers the strongside hook area.

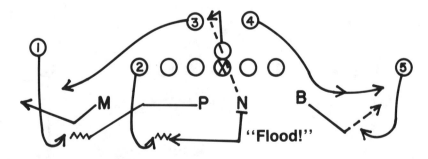

Diagram 3.49a   When both backs release, and the quarterback drops back and looks to the strong side, Nasty (ILB) slides strong.

If the quarterback "looks weak," Nasty slides over and covers the weakside hook area. Diagrams 3.49a and b show the inside linebacker (Nasty) dropping straight back versus an "all-out" pass pattern and covering the strongside or weakside hook area, depending on which side the quarterback looks to.

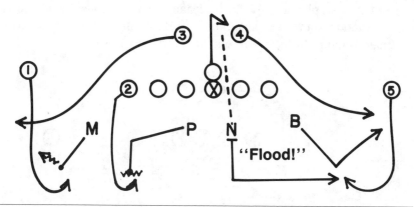

Diagram 3.49b   When both backs release, and the quarterback drops back and looks to the weak side, Nasty (ILB) slides weak.

Linebacker Responsibilities Versus the Sprint-Out Pass

The linebackers' reactions to the ball moving outside of the offensive tackle's area depend largely on the defensive coverage call they are in at the time. When in the base defensive coverage (Omaha), the outside linebacker to the side that the ball is coming to aggressively attacks and attempts to contain the passer. His rule is "Ball comes, you come." The technique he uses to execute his responsibilities is the same as that described versus the run.

The standard reactions to sprint-out or to roll-out pass action for the remaining linebackers include the onside-inside linebacker's aggressive attempt to get to the quarterback through the offensive tackle's area. In the base 44 set, your defense is designed around the assumption that the offensive tackle has to block down on the defensive tackle when the ball gets outside of the B gap. This factor was very important to the validity of the defense versus the run and is likewise important versus the defense's ability to attack the sprint-out pass action.

When the offensive tackle blocks down on the defensive tackle, a lane is created for the inside linebacker to get to the quarterback. This lane is referred to as a *scrape-hole,* and the action of the inside linebacker as *scraping* to the ball. The backside-inside linebacker checks his onside A gap and drives to the onside hook area. The backside-outside linebacker shuffles backward for five yards, looking for a throwback, etc., and then pursues the pass play through the backside "seam" created by the secondary's rotation to the ball. Diagram 3.50 shows the linebacker's Omaha coverage rotation to the sprint-out or roll-out pass play.

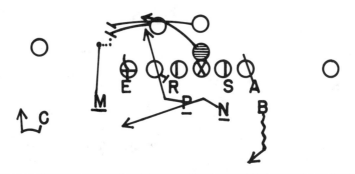

Diagram 3.50   Maco (SOLB) comes under control one yard underneath and one yard outside the lead blocker. Panther (IRLB) attacks the quarterback from a position half-a-man behind the ball.

Linebacker Pursuit Adjustments

Variations in the linebackers' pursuit angles and rotation schemes must be used to compensate for the numerous situations that arise. Offensive formations, personnel, down and distance, field position, etc., can all influence what coverage, adjustment, or scheme you choose to go with.

"Mayday" Coverage

A *Mayday* call means that the secondary will not rotate up to the onside flat zone when the ball moves outside of the offensive tackle's position. This makes it necessary for the outside linebacker to cover that area when the ball comes his way. The remainder of the linebacker's pursuit angles are the same as with the base Omaha rotation. Diagram 3.51 demonstrates the linebacker's pursuit versus the sprint-out pass with a "Mayday" call.

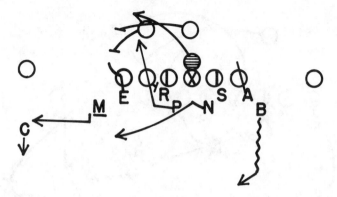

Diagram 3.51 When play action comes to his side, Maco (SOLB) quickly moves to the outside flat zone or strong flat area, rather than attacking the ball, as he would under Omaha coverage.

"Walk-Off," "In," and "Back" Adjustments

When your outside linebackers find themselves back off the line of scrimmage because of any of these adjustments, they *will not* attack the sprint-out or roll-out pass action when it comes to their side, even though they may be in Omaha coverage. From these deep positions (about six yards off the line of scrimmage), the outside linebackers cannot effectively come up and attack the quarterback on his sprint-out pass. If they attempt to do so, they usually end up in another "no-man's land"—where they can neither help against the pass nor get to the passer. If the defense is in an Omaha coverage, the outside linebacker will "squat" in the curl area when the ball moves to his side. He helps defend against the wide receiver's slant and curl patterns and gives delayed support to quarterback sweeps, options, etc. Diagram 3.52 demonstrates this predicament—when the outside linebacker is in a Walk-off position because of a wide-slot alignment (assume the defense is utilizing an "Omaha" call).

"Lay-Back" Adjustment

You may want to call off your onside-inside linebacker's scrape to the ball for various reasons. It may be that he is not getting to the ball in time to be of defensive help. Or, you may need him to cover the wide receiver's slant or curl patterns. Often he will be in a better position to help defend against more plays if he does not aggressively attack the ball. You might call it more of a "bend, but do not break" adjustment. Diagram 3.53 shows all

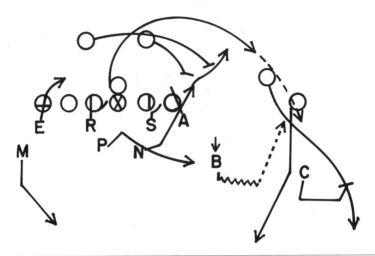

Diagram 3.52   Brutus (WOLB) squats in the curl area before eventually coming up and supporting against the quarterback's run.

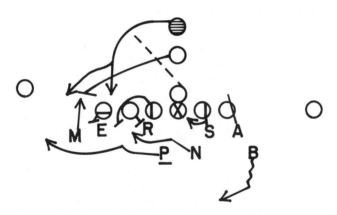

Diagram 3.53   Maco (SOLB) reacts to the "Omaha" call by attacking the ball, but the inside linebackers now pursue laterally to get in a better position for covering passes and wide running plays.

the linebackers pursuing the sweep action from a "44 *Lay-back*–Omaha" call.

"Plug" Adjustment

As shown previously, sometimes the opponent's blocking schemes will open up a lane for your backside-inside linebacker to get to the ball from a position behind the offensive blockers. The *Plug* call would allow you to put pressure on the outside play from the inside, and still have the onside-inside linebacker pursuing laterally down the line of scrimmage. Diagram 3.54 shows the 44 Plug-Omaha stopping the opponent's off-tackle play.

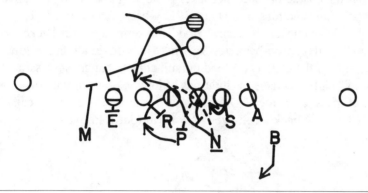

Diagram 3.54 The backside-inside linebacker aggressively attacks the off-tackle play by penetrating through gaps created by certain offensive blocking schemes.

"Slug" Adjustment

Often, you may want to send all three linebackers to the side of the action to the ball. The *Slug* call tells both inside linebackers to attack the side of the ball. The onside-inside linebacker attacks through his scrape-hole, and the backside-inside linebacker attacks through his plug-hole. This call may also be used without the outside linebacker being involved by having him in a deep position or a Mayday adjustment. Diagram 3.55 illustrates the linebackers aggressively attacking with a "44 Slug-Omaha" call.

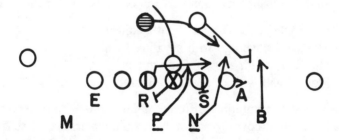

Diagram 3.55 Both inside linebackers aggressively attack the play action through the available scrape-holes.

"Flood" Adjustment

The linebacker pursuit package includes the ability for all three onside pursuing linebackers to pursue wide plays laterally and not attack over the line of scrimmage. This adjustment is called with Mayday coverage that has the onside-outside linebacker protecting the outside flat area. The "Flood" call is nothing more than a "Lay-back" call with Mayday coverage. We have chosen the term "flood" to remind the linebackers of the "Flood" call on drop-back passes, where they cover all three short zones to the side of the call. The Flood pursuit adjustment does the same thing. "Flood" calls are made in situations of long yardage or when you expect a short pass or screen. Diagram 3.56 shows a "Flood" call (or a "Mayday–Lay-back" call) versus a sprint-out flare pass.

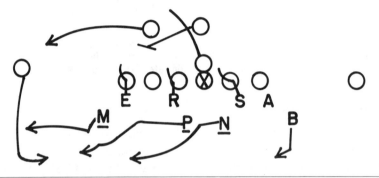

Diagram 3.56 With a "Mayday" call, all three onside linebackers move laterally, with depth, to the playside action.

If you review the section of the book on linebacker alignment adjustments, you see that certain alignment adjustments go hand in hand with certain pursuit adjustments. Some of the obvious combinations are

- a "Lay-back" call with an "Out" adjustment
- a "Mayday" coverage with a "Plug" call
- a "Slug" call with an "Up" alignment
- a "Flood" call with a "Back" alignment

When you start combining different adjustments with different alignments and different coverages, you have quite an arsenal of schemes to play around with when devising your championship game plan versus the Massillon-Moeller Maneaters.

Chapter 4

Developing the "Front-Eight's" Support System: The Defensive Secondary

The Super Split's three-deep secondary players are separated from their front-eight teammates not only by alignment, but by assignment and methodology as well. They really are a breed apart. You want your front-eight "infantry men" up in the trenches, anxiously awaiting the siege of the enemy ball carrier. By contrast, you want the proficient secondary players in the background, supporting their front-line soldiers like pilots in the Strategic Air Command. Their primary responsibilities are to deny the long plays and support the front-eight in case of breakdown. We help the secondary keep their priorities in perspective by reemphasizing to them: (1) Don't get beat deep! (2) Don't get beat deep! (3) Don't get beat deep! This may sound like a negative assignment, but it gets the point across. The secondary defenders must keep aggressiveness limited to attacking the ball when it is in the air and attacking the ball carrier after he has passed the line of scrimmage. Nothing is more devastating to a defensive effort than to battle toe-to-toe with the opponent, only to have a secondary member "doze off" for an instant and let his receiver slip behind him for the game-winning touchdown. The secondary defenders must understand their role within the defensive plan and philosophy.

The Secondary's Alignment and Stance Specifics

All three secondary defenders will utilize a similar presnap stance, which contrasts with the more aggressive linebacker stances in a number of ways. The defensive backs' stance must serve almost the opposite function as that of the linebacker. Whereas the linebacker's stance must help him move aggressively as well as quickly forward and laterally, the three-deep defenders need only to retreat on the snap of the ball. They also need a bigger picture of the offense's initial movement, which requires a taller stance. Consequently, your defensive backs assume a two-point stance, with their outside foot back and both feet pointing at a 45° angle to the side line and the line of scrimmage. The safety uses a similar stance, facing at a 45° angle to the wide side of the field or to the two-receiver side. All three have most of their weight resting on their back foot and are just slightly crouched. They maintain the basics of a good stance (back straight, feet shoulder-width apart, toes pointing in same direction), but they are visibly more relaxed and loose than their front-eight counterparts. Diagram 4.1 illustrates the foot placement of the three secondary players.

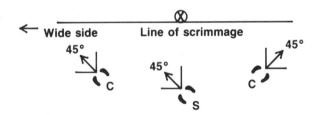

Diagram 4.1   The feet of the three secondary players do not face the receiver, but rather are in a position that allows the defender to immediately open up and run backward on the snap of the ball.

The secondary's alignment positions and their adjustments to the various offensive formations are taught first by having them align versus a standard two-tight-end, full-house offensive formation. The cornerbacks are given a "rule-of-thumb" explanation of where to line up. This casual approach is by design, because many extenuating circumstances may alter or influence a cornerback's decision concerning alignment depth or width. Versus the two-tight-end formation the cornerbacks would align approximately four yards deep and four yards outside the tight end's position. The safety is also given rule-of-thumb directions; he aligns as deep from the ball as the cornerbacks are wide from the ball. His lateral positioning is referred to as "splitting the difference between the two cornerbacks." As the offensive receivers move out wider, the cornerbacks get deeper but align closer laterally. With the receivers split ten yards from the ball, the cornerbacks would be approximately seven yards deep and maintain a one-yard outside advantage. As the receivers split out to as much as a seventeen-yard distance (hash mark to hash mark) from the ball, the cornerback would reach his maximum depth of nine or ten yards and would move to an inside (two or three yards) position advantage. Diagrams 4.2a, b, and c illustrate these adjustments, with the safety continuing to be as deep as the cornerbacks are wide, while splitting the distance between the two.

The extenuating circumstances that necessitate alignment by rule-of-thumb include such factors as the opponent's speed, the defender's speed, lateral or vertical field position, field conditions, down and distance, the

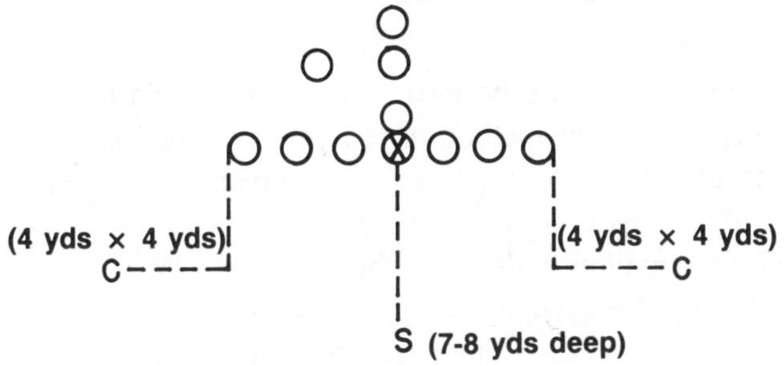

Diagram 4.2a Secondary alignment against two tight ends.

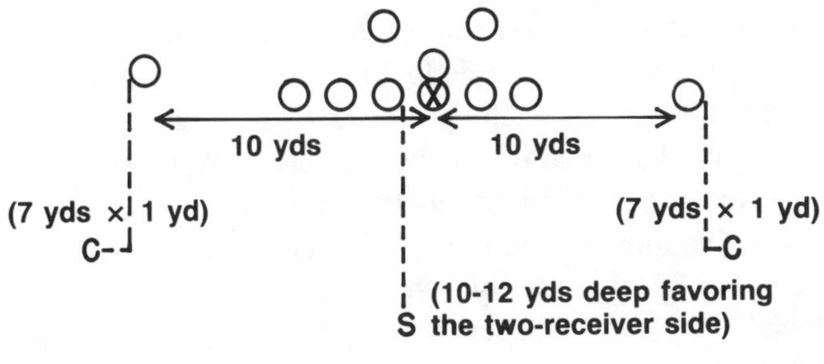

Diagram 4.2b Secondary alignment against ten-yard splits.

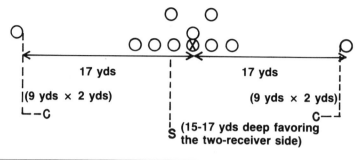

Diagram 4.2c   Secondary alighment against seventeen (or more)-yard splits.

score, and the time remaining. Obviously, "football sense" will determine much of the secondary's ultimate alignment position. As will be shown, some of the defense's alignment and coverage adjustments will require adjustments in stances as well as techniques.

Secondary Responsibilities and Technique Specifics

You may find this section the most controversial relative to what most coaches accept as proper method or technique for defensive backs when retreating to cover their deep zones. As a coach, I am well aware that the technique we teach our defensive backs is not the one taught by most American high school or college coaches. But this *straight-line* technique, which I have taught for twenty years, has been very successful in helping our defensive backs perform their responsibilities. In other words, you may be able to pick it apart theoretically, but pragmatically, it works.

The straight-line technique reduces the skills the defensive back has to learn by one, that being the back-pedal or backward shuffle. Instead, on the snap of the ball the defensive back runs backward (his feet facing away from the line of scrimmage) while looking over his shoulder to the quarterback and the ball. This technique was taught to me by my coaches at the University of Washington, way back in the early 1960s. I believe that my coach, Jim Owens, brought this technique with him either from the University of Oklahoma, where he played under Coach Bud Wilkinson, or from Texas A&M University, where he was an assistant coach under Paul "Bear" Bryant. Whichever was the case, it came with good credentials.

The straight-line technique allows the defensive back to run on the snap of the ball. Running is faster than shuffling, and that is the big advantage of this technique. It may not seem like an important difference, but it appears that most high school secondary players get beat deep because the offensive receiver is able to close down the cushion or distance between the two very quickly when the secondary man is back-pedaling. As the distance between the two gets less and less, the defensive back eventually has to decide when to open up and run with the receiver. Because the receiver is running full speed ahead during this moment of decision, the defender might easily miscalculate the offensive man's position and speed and end up getting beat deep. This vital defensive decision is made during a moment that is confusing and frantic because of play fakery, the receiver's moves, and all of the other simultaneous action. This scenario leads many times to the defensive backs being beat deep!

The strength of the back-pedal technique is that the defender's shoulders are kept square to the line of scrimmage, enabling him not only to see more of the field, but also to stop quicker and to break in either direction versus short passes. At the major college and professional levels this advantage is vital because of the offense's ability to beat you down the field with the short passing game. In nearly all high school football contests you can delegate the opponent's short passing game to the linebackers (including secondary players who have rotated up for short zone coverage). The secondary can concentrate on protecting the deep zones and on coming up and making good, hard tackles on the receivers who catch passes underneath them. Most coaches would agree that it won't be your opponent's short passing game that defeats you. Rather, it will be a strong, ball-control running game, the long runs, the long passes, or the opponent's superior field-control kicking game that will probably be the major factors involved in your defeat. The straight-line technique may prove to be a little weaker versus the opponent's short passes, but this is well outweighed by your secondary's improved abilities versus the long, game-winning bomb.

Straight-Line Technique

The *straight-line* technique is taught simply by having players run down a yard line while looking back over their shoulders at the passer. If they are looking over their left shoulder and the passer looks to his right (as if to pass the ball in that direction), the defensive backs pivot on their back foot (always keeping their eyes on the passer) so that they continue to run down the line, but are now looking over their right shoulder. An important coaching point is the need for the defender to keep his shoulders over his knees. This keeps the defensive back in a lower, crouched running form, which enables him to stop and move forward quicker. Some of the drills to improve the player's use of this technique are described in chapter 11.

On the snap of the ball, all three secondary men begin to retreat to their respective pass coverage zones. They do *not* shuffle, but instead open up with the back foot and take a minimum of three *cushion* steps before making any pursuit decisions. Normally, they will be facing to the outside, looking over the inside shoulder to the ball. Players should always take the cushion steps, no matter what offensive action occurs at the snap of the ball. This is to get your secondary defenders moving backward, so they will not get sucked in on a run fake that ends up being a deep pass.

Shade Technique

Versus the drop-back pass the secondary utilizes what we refer to as the *shade* technique. The term "shade" refers to the defender's facing his chest in the direction of the offensive receiver in his coverage area. You want your defensive back to do this only when the quarterback is looking to the defender's side of the field. When the quarterback is looking away, the defensive back will face the direction the quarterback is looking.

Visualize a defensive back retreating to cover his deep zone, with a receiver just to his outside. When the quarterback looks in the direction of this receiver the defensive back pivots so that his chest faces, or shades, the receiver. If the quarterback is looking to the other side of the field, the defensive back also faces his chest to the other side of the field. The purpose of shading is to allow the defender to move faster in the direction

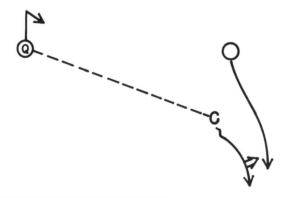

Diagram 4.3a   The quarterback looks toward the defender's side, with the receiver in an outside position. The defensive back's chest would be facing outside toward the receiver.

he is initially facing, rather than having to pivot first and then move toward the receiver and the ball. Remember, the defensive back is looking at the quarterback while seeing the receiver in his peripheral vision. Diagrams 4.3a, b, and c illustrate this technique in the three possible situations.

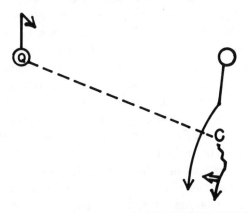

Diagram 4.3b The quarterback looks toward the defender's side, with the receiver in an inside position. The defensive back's chest would be facing inside toward the receiver.

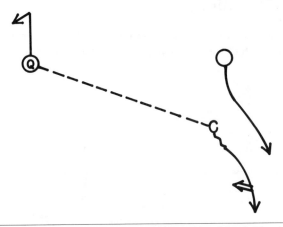

Diagram 4.3c The quarterback looks toward the far side of the field, with the receiver in an outside position to the defender. The defensive back's chest would be facing the far side of the field.

Treading-Water Technique

Treading-water is perhaps one of the most important techniques for a good secondary player to learn. It is not so much a technique as simply the defender anticipating what a receiver might do and then preparing himself for what might occur. Two of the most common patterns a receiver uses to beat a defender deep are the *sideline-and-go* and the *hook-and-go*. Both routes lure the defender into changing his momentum from a backward to a forward motion. Once a defender's momentum starts forward in his intention to break up the short pass, he is easy prey for a receiver who continues his route deep. The treading-water technique tells your defensive back that when a receiver in his area breaks off his initial course to run an apparent short pattern, the back should *not* stop and move forward to cover the man. You don't want the defensive back to continue speeding backward, becoming further separated from the receiver, but you don't want him to change gears and move aggressively forward before the ball has been thrown either. What you do want is for him to slow down his retreat until he is merely moving his feet in place, maintaining his three-yard cushion on the receiver. If the ball is thrown, he then accelerates at the shortest angle to the ball, reaching for the ball with both hands and eyes. If the receiver continues his pattern deep after the short fake, the defender simply resumes his backward straight-line retreat while covering his deep zone. Diagrams 4.4a and b demonstrate the treading-water technique versus the two most common "sucker" routes.

Look-In Technique

The *look-in* technique is another we use (quite often) that might face abuse from a sophisticated college passing attack. It is used when the offense

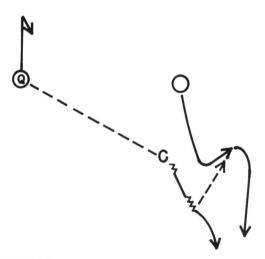

Diagram 4.4a   The wide receiver runs a sideline-and-go route, with the cornerback using the treading-water technique to successfully defend the pattern. The dotted lines from the cornerback to the receiver indicate that the defender attacks the ball if it is thrown at that time.

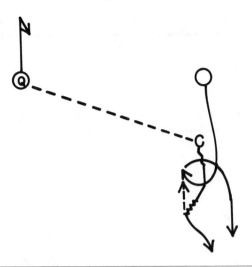

Diagram 4.4b   The wide receiver runs a hook-and-go route, and the cornerback defends with the treading-water technique.

splits their wide receivers out so far that the cornerback becomes un-comfortable in his regular stance (facing outside and looking back at the ball over his inside shoulder). The look-in technique allows him to face inside in his presnap position. The defender can utilize this stance from the same depth he would take with the normal stance, but normally he will move up as close as three to four yards in front of the wide receiver. The look-in technique is used almost always when opposing a team that throws a lot of look-in (slant or short post) patterns. The cornerback using the look-in technique will align on the wide receiver's outside shoulder, facing directly in at the ball in a stance perpendicular to the line of scrim-mage. On the snap of the ball he will take his customary cushion steps while looking at the quarterback and seeing the wide receiver in his peripheral vision. If the wide receiver releases off the line of scrimmage to the inside, the defensive back (still looking at the quarterback) runs with the receiver for four or five yards to take away the quick slant pass. If the ball is thrown he goes through the receiver, with both hands and eyes going for the ball. If the ball is not thrown in those first five yards, the defensive back just continues back and assumes his normal coverage. If the receiver releases outside (goes behind the defensive back), your corner-back moves to the outside as he retreats, enough that he can still see the wide receiver peripherally. Your cornerback will be able to see the wide receiver when he releases outside as long as he maintains at least a three-yard cushion. If the sideline is nearby, the defensive back can squeeze the receiver into it by continuing to widen his position as he covers his

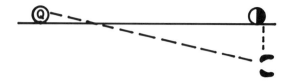

Diagram 4.5a   When using the look-in technique, the cornerback should be three to four yards deep, with foot position and alignment as shown.

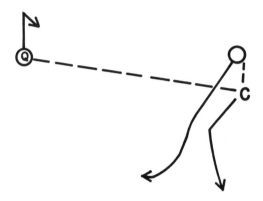

Diagram 4.5b   When the wide receiver releases inside, the cornerback runs with the receiver for five yards to take away the slant pass and then proceeds to his deep coverage area.

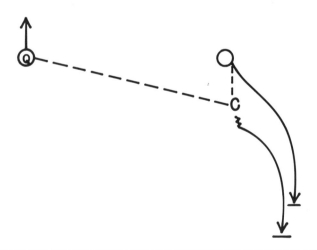

Diagram 4.5c   To defend against a receiver who releases outside of him, the cornerback uses the look-in technique, gaining width as he retreats to his deep coverage zone. The cornerback must maintain the three-yard cushion to be able to use peripheral vision to see the receiver.

deep third. Diagrams 4.5a, b, and c illustrate the look-in technique's alignment and reaction to the two typical wide receiver releases.

A primary pattern you will have to work against if you use the look-in technique is a combination pattern with the outside receiver running the short post and the inside receiver running the wheel or fly route. (This pattern can be tough against any coverage.) The cornerback has to retreat the five yards with the wide receiver's inside route and then continue back and cover his deep third versus the inside receiver's wheel route. Versus a wide-slot offensive formation this pattern is not quite as difficult, because the outside linebacker is positioned right in front of the wide receiver's short post pattern (see Diagram 4.6).

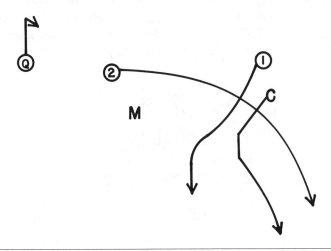

Diagram 4.6   The cornerback's coverage of both the wide receiver's short inside route and the inside receiver's deep outside route.

Raider Technique

The *Raider* technique is an adjustment to a formation (or it can be a call) that releases the cornerback from his rule of taking three cushion steps on the snap of the ball. When the cornerback is aligned against a tight-end-only side, it is automatic for him to alter his normal stance to one similar to the look-in stance, which is perpendicular to the line and facing in at the quarterback. From this position he will key through the tight end's block to the action of the near-back. If the tight end blocks the man over him and the action of the near-back is coming his way, the cornerback immediately attacks the line of scrimmage. The Raider technique is always used in conjunction with a "Squeeze" call, which moves the outside linebacker into a position covering the offensive C gap. This means that the cornerback is the first defender to come up and turn in plays run to his side. He actually assumes the outside linebacker's previous duty. This call allows the outside linebacker to protect, or help defend, the off-tackle area before pursuing plays going to the outside. As you can see, this adjustment gives strength in numbers versus off-tackle and wide plays directed toward the offense's tight-end-only side.

We suggest you hold off teaching this technique to younger athletes. Our reason for this is wanting our cornerbacks to first develop the firm habit of taking the required cushion steps at the snap of the ball. If the Raider technique is taught too soon, the defensive back does not acquire the desired habit necessary to perform his fundamental defensive rule, in which retreat is his initial movement. Diagram 4.7 illustrates the Raider technique along with Omaha coverage, which has the safety rotating to the side of the ball. The outside linebacker has been squeezed inside, which strengthens the defense in the off-tackle area.

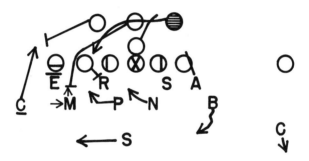

Diagram 4.7 A 44 set with Raider technique and Omaha coverage.

Man-to-Man Technique

In developing our defensive philosophy, we have elected to concentrate on the development of zone coverages. Having chosen this priority, we have kept the man-to-man coverage technique as simple as possible. Man coverage (referred to in our system as *Kansas* coverage, because when a game goes into overtime, called the Kansas Plan, your team would normally be in a goal-line, man-to-man defense) is called when you want to blitz two or more of your linebackers or when you are in goal-line defense.

The *Man-to-Man* technique is first taught to the defensive backs versus wide receivers. When Kansas coverage is called, the cornerbacks align on the inside shoulder of the wide receiver, tight to the line of scrimmage, facing out at a 45° angle. They assume a much more aggressive stance (lower, feet wider, arms and elbows inside, ready to deliver a blow) and concentrate entirely on the wide receiver. As the receiver moves off the line of scrimmage, the defender jams him to the outside, obstructing his release as much as possible. The cornerback must not let the receiver get to his immediate inside. As the receiver releases to the outside, the cornerback runs with him, sticking to his inside shoulder, and reads the end's hat and shoulders for the signal that he is changing direction or attempting to catch the ball. When the receiver looks back for the ball, the cornerback imitates his move, also looking back for the ball, while he leans into the receiver's position and goes for the ball himself.

Sometimes the defensive backs or linebackers are unable to take an inside position on the man they are to cover man-to-man, for example, when they have to cover a tight end. If the end is already covered by a defensive player (the defensive end in a normal set), the defensive back would have to align to the outside. From this position, he would make contact with the tight end when he released off the line of scrimmage from an outside-in position. The cornerback would attempt to maintain this outside leverage, while disrupting the end's release. If the tight end did manage to escape to the outside, the defender would cover him from an inside-out advantage, as he would versus a wide receiver.

Whenever a defensive player has to cover an offensive man from a head-up position, he will, as we football coaches say, "get right in the man's face." From this intimidating position the defender tries to defeat the end's block or to obstruct his release off the line of scrimmage. When the receiver does gain release to one side or the other, the defender must maintain his inside (or outside) advantage. Diagrams 4.8a, b, c, and d illustrate the Man-to-Man technique in four different situations.

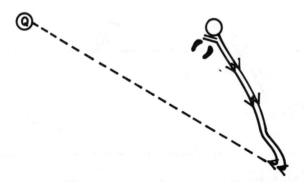

Diagram 4.8a   The cornerback's foot position when using a Man-to-Man technique against a wide receiver. As the receiver runs a deep route, the cornerback runs with him on his inside shoulder. The cornerback leans into the receiver and looks back for the ball when the receiver turns for the reception. By jamming the receiver in this way, the cornerback forces an outside release.

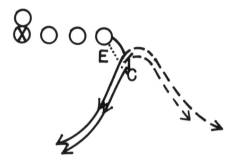

Diagram 4.8b The cornerback covers a tight end who is covered by a defensive end. When the tight end releases outside, the cornerback jams him to the inside and maintains that position while the tight end runs an inside route. If the tight end breaks outside, the cornerback assumes an inside-out position.

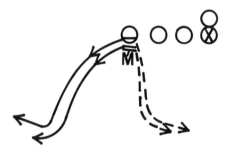

Diagram 4.8c When covering a tight end from a head-up position, Maco (SOLB) jams him, holds up his release, and then maintains an insude-out position as the tight end eventually releases to the outside. If the tight end breaks to the inside, Maco assumes an outside-in position.

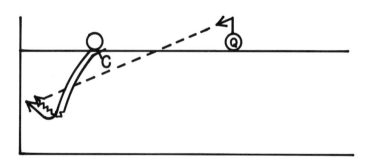

Diagram 4.8d In Man-to-Man coverage on the goal line, the cornerbacks break underneath the wide receiver's flat route when the receiver looks back for the ball.

Chapter 5

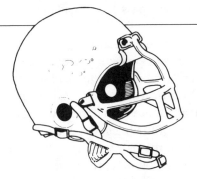

The "Seven-Spokes" Pass Coverages and Play Pursuit

Although the *seven-spokes'* various coverages and pursuit angles comple-ment the four-down linemen's run-stopping and pass-rushing efforts, the two groups' assignments are almost entirely independent of each other. This means that the defensive linemen need not be aware of any of the zone coverage calls or adjustments. The only time the defensive line needs to be involved with the seven-spokes' game is when the linebackers are blitzing; then the linemen have to know which gap they are supposed to hit. This separation of group responsibilities enables the seven-spokes to isolate themselves more often in practice and to concentrate on improv-ing their skills related to coverages and pursuit angles.

"Omaha" Coverage

The fundamental manner in which the seven-spokes react to the type or direction of the offensive play is directed by the methods outlined in the defense's base coverage, Omaha. This basic, three-deep zone coverage responds to the movement or rotation of the offensive play. When the ball carrier retreats straight back (drop-back pass), the linebackers retreat to their respective drop-back pass zones, and the three-deep each cover their deep third of the field. When the ball carrier (or just the ball) moves toward one sideline or the other, the seven-spokes rotate to the ball, which results in their covering different zones or performing different responsibilities. The imaginary boundary lines that the ball must cross before the spokes rotate are vertical lines drawn from the inside hip of the offensive tackles. If the ball stays inside these boundaries, the defense does not rotate. If the ball goes past one of the lines, the defense rotates up to the ball. The term *Omaha* relates to the ball moving outside of the offensive tackle's position, in which case the defense rotates.

"Omaha" Coverage Versus a Drop-Back Pass

When the quarterback drops straight back or to a position inside or behind either offensive tackle, the defensive safety yells, "Deep, deep," signaling to the other defensive backs (and the linebackers if they can hear him) that the ball is inside the tackles and that they should cover their deep one-third zones. The linebackers would be dropping to their coverage areas (as described in the linebacker section). Diagram 5.1 illustrates the quarterback dropping back inside the tackle's area and the seven-spokes reacting within the Omaha coverage design.

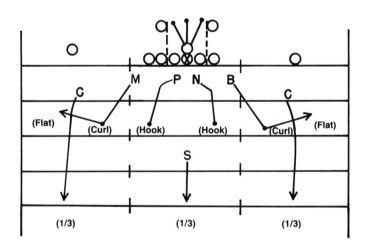

Diagram 5.1   As the quarterback drops back inside the tackle's area and the seven-spokes react within the Omaha coverage design, the defensive backs retreat down the middle of each zone.

Your linebackers and secondary players must realize that the field distribution responsibilities stay the same, regardless of where the ball is aligned from hash mark to hash mark. You teach them not to "cover air"; if there is a receiver in the area that they are responsible for, they must get in a position to cover him. In Diagram 5.2, the ball is on the hash mark and the quarterback is dropping back to pass. Notice how the linebacker and the three-deep have to alter their retreat angle to get to their respective zones.

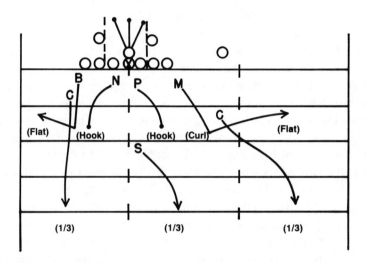

Diagram 5.2 The linebackers and secondary defenders scramble to cover their areas of field responsibility. The defenders at the wide side of the field must retreat at very flat angles to reach their areas.

"Omaha" Coverage Versus a Sprint-Out Pass

Offensive sweep, roll-out, or sprint-out action versus your Omaha coverage has the onside-outside linebacker aggressively attacking the lead blocker to contain the play. The onside-inside linebacker attacks the ball carrier through his scrape-hole, while the two backside linebackers check their gap responsibilities before getting into the proper pursuit angles. These linebacker reactions to the ball being run toward the flanks have been illustrated and described elsewhere (see chapter 3, "Inside Linebacker Reads and Reactions Versus the Run" and "Outside Linebacker Reads and Reactions Versus the Run").

In Omaha coverage, the three-deep secondary react to the ball moving outside of the tackle's area in a manner very similar to that of the linebackers.

The cornerback to the side of the action, after taking his preliminary cushion steps, levels off and covers the onside (ten to fifteen yards deep) flat zone. The safety is now responsible to cover the onside deep one-third area between the hash mark and the sideline. The backside cornerback will get at least five yards depth before covering the back two-thirds of the field.

There are some very important coaching points for the proper execution of the Omaha coverage rotation. First, the onside cornerback when leveling off has to square up to the line of scrimmage and get to an outside shoulder position on the wide receiver. From this position he will thwart the receiver's unobstructed, deep-outside "go" pattern. The defensive back attempts to alter the end's intended route, so that he is forced to run the pattern inside of the cornerback's position. This makes the safety's responsibility of covering the outside deep area a lot easier, because he is not required to stretch himself so far to cover the wide receiver.

When rotating to cover the outside deep third of the field, the safety must first check the wide receiver's pattern to see if he is releasing toward the inside short post area. If this pattern is materializing, the safety must come under control (treading water), not flying off to cover the outside third. If the ball is thrown to the wide receiver's short post pattern, the safety is in a position to defend. Once the threat of the pattern's completion is past, the safety continues to his area of primary responsibility. If the offensive play evolves from a position near the middle of the hash marks, the safety's rotation route on an "Omaha" call has him retreat down the onside hash mark. The backside cornerback rotates to a position that takes him down the backside hash mark while covering the back two-thirds of the field. Diagram 5.3 demonstrates a base 44 set, Omaha coverage, versus a sprint-out pass play.

Certain circumstances that occur with a defensive coverage that rotates to the offense's action should be discussed. One of the most important facets of Omaha coverage success is the ability of the defense to know when (and when not) to rotate to the ball. The spokes are taught to rotate when the ball gets outside the imaginary line drawn from the offensive tackles' inside hip. The decision, though, is not always that cut-and-dried. Many times the quarterback and backfield will appear to be going outside but pull up at the last second behind their offensive tackles. This is usually referred to as a semiroll or side-pocket position. You can imagine what would happen if some of the spokes rotated and some didn't; there would be a large uncovered area in the secondary.

Much of the responsibility for proper rotation reaction is given to the safety, who has the best view of the action. His decisions as to when to call "Deep, deep" and when to make the "Omaha" call (which informs

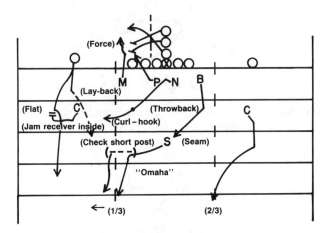

Diagram 5.3   The seven-spokes' basic rotation coverage against the offense's quick attack to the flank.

the rest of the spokes that the ball is outside of the tackle area and that they are to rotate) are aided by knowledge of the opponent's play tendencies. The safety should study opponents' films and scouting reports so that he almost will know beforehand when and when not to rotate. The outside linebackers also need a good idea of which offensive play actions are considered rotating plays before entering each contest.

The safety can become very proficient at calling rotations by learning to read basic play actions. When initial play action is aggressively attacking the flanks, he can make the "Omaha" call very quickly. The safety will also learn to pick up keys such as the quarterback's angle of retreat and the movement of the remaining backs. Diagrams 5.4a, b, and c illustrate play actions that can tip the safety's decision about whether to call for the rotation.

The safety should not be led to think that his decisions on calling for

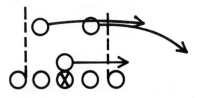

Diagram 5.4a   Noticing fast action with all three backs, the safety can make a quick "Omaha" call.

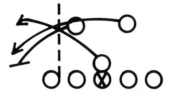

Diagram 5.4b A sprint-out pass action with the quarterback releasing at a shallow angle and both backs leading tips the safety to make a quick rotation call.

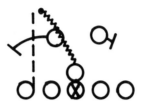

Diagram 5.4c If the quarterback releases deeper and runs under more control than for a sprint-out pass, and the fullback blocks to the back side, this tips the safety that the play is semi-sprint-out. The safety would therefore call out "Deep, deep."

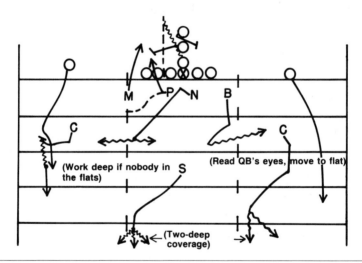

Diagram 5.5 The safety has mistakenly called "Omaha," and the quarterback sets up behind the tackle in a side-pocket position. The safety could call "Deep, deep" after seeing the quarterback set up, but either way the defenders cover the drop-back pass from their rotated position.

rotation coverage will make or break the defense's success. What is most important to the defense is that all seven-spokes act as a unit—either all rotate or none rotate. Diagram 5.5 demonstrates this axiom with a semi-sprint-out play in which the safety prematurely called for spoke rotation.

As you can see, all that occurs is that the secondary ends up in a two-deep look, requiring the backside cornerback and outside linebacker to fight back and cover their outside areas.

Diagrams 5.6a, b, c, and d illustrate some of the sprint-out pass action patterns that are particularly difficult for the rotation coverage to defend and give coaching points to help the defenders defeat the patterns.

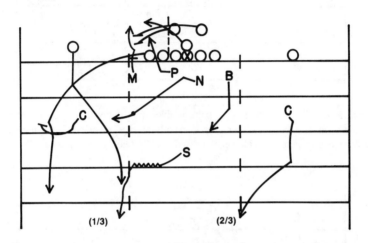

Diagram 5.6a   One of the most difficult patterns to cover with the Omaha rotation is the combination short post and wheel pattern (shown in Diagram 4.6). This pattern requires the cornerback to jam the inside receiver's deep route and the safety to check the wide receiver's inside pattern before covering his deep outside third area.

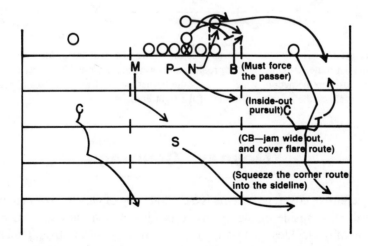

Diagram 5.6b   Another combination pattern that stretches the rotation coverage is the corner and flare patterns run to the weak side. The safety really has to hustle!

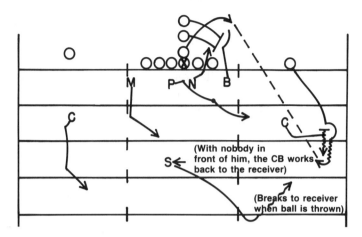

Diagram 5.6c   The outside "seam" pattern gives the rotation coverage problems when run to the weak side because the safety is usually aligned favoring the strong side. The cornerback has to jam the wide receiver and shuffle back with the "seam" route.

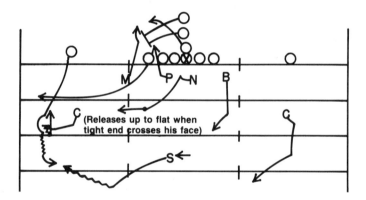

Diagram 5.6d   The "seam" pattern run to the strong side, with the inside receiver running the flat route, presents another problem to the rotating defense. The safety is aligned a little closer to the action, which enables the cornerback to leave the "seam" pattern earlier to attack the underneath route of the tight end.

"Mayday" Coverage

This defensive coverage scheme is a carbon copy of Omaha coverage when the ball stays inside of the offensive tackles. When the ball does move outside of the tackles' position, Mayday coverage differs from Omaha in that the spokes do not rotate as drastically. In a *Mayday* call, the onside-outside linebacker and cornerback do not rotate up to the ball. The cornerback instead continues to cover his deep outside third area as he does versus a drop-back pass. The outside linebacker, rather than moving up to force the ball inside, sprints outside to cover the onside flat area. Because the onside cornerback remains in his deep outside zone, the safety is released from the deep outside third responsibility on sprint-out pass action. "Mayday" is a very sound coverage call as a "prevent" defense against your opponent's last-ditch efforts. It is also very useful versus an opponent with two fast receivers placed wide to opposite sides, making it difficult for your safety to cover both outside deep zones when the ball flows in their direction. The coverage is not as aggressive as with the "Omaha" call, but it is a stronger and safer coverage versus roll-out offenses that like to attack the outside passing zones. Diagram 5.7 illustrates Mayday coverage action versus a spread-out offensive set. Notice how the safety, who "mirrors" the quarterback's flow as he gains depth, ends up in the deep flat area underneath the defensive cornerback's position. When the offense comes out and lines up in a formation with everybody spread out, your defense would normally adjust with a "Mayday" call.

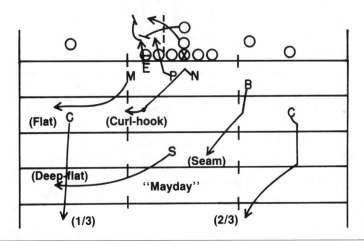

Diagram 5.7 Without the outside linebacker forcing the sprint-out, the defensive end and onside-inside linebacker have to pick up the slack (Mayday coverage).

"Lucy"/"Rosey" Coverage

This coverage adjustment can be very useful; it has your spokes using Omaha coverage if the ball goes to one side and Mayday coverage for the other side. The coverage normally is referred to as *Weak Mayday;*

the *Lucy* call signifies that Mayday is being run to the left and the *Rosey* call indicates that Mayday coverage is being run to the right. "Weak Mayday" alludes to the fact that your defense will utilize the Mayday coverage to the opponent's (or field's) weak side and will cover the strong side with the base Omaha coverage. The biggest advantage of this coverage is that it allows your safety to "cheat" way over to the side of the Omaha coverage, because he does not have to cover the deep outside third to the other side. Although this coverage is usually called to the weak side, in some situations you may want to call *Strong Mayday,* cover the offense's strongside action with Mayday coverage, and roll up to the weakside action with your Omaha rotation. Diagram 5.8a illustrates a "Lucy" call with the quarterback rolling to the left; the dotted lines show him going to the right. Diagram 5.8b demonstrates a "Rosey" call, with schematic drawings showing the quarterback moving in both directions.

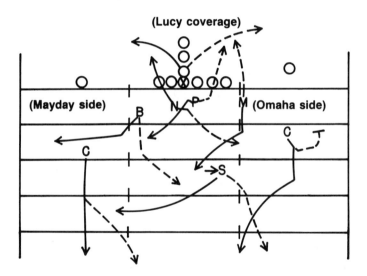

Diagram 5.8a   When using Lucy coverage, the safety can move over quite a distance to the right because there is Mayday coverage to the left.

"Buckeye" Coverage

This coverage, which rotates one of the secondary backs up to cover a short passing zone before the snap of the ball, would be considered a major adjustment to your eight-man front, three-deep defense. In many situations you feel that you can adequately cover the deep passing zones with

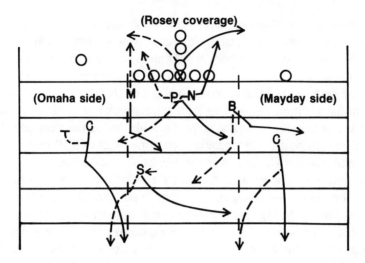

Diagram 5.8b Weak Mayday coverage was signaled in by the coaches. When the safety sees that the offensive formation is strong left, he calls "Rosey."

just two defensive backs. This allows you to put one extra defender in the short passing zones, conveniently fortifying the split defense's base coverage, which has nobody assigned to the middle short zone. The two-deep/five-under *Buckeye* coverage is a great change-up coverage for a defense that is normally stronger in the deep zones and a little more vulnerable to skillful short passing attacks. This is a great coverage versus the second down or versus third-down long yardage situations. On third down, with the offense needing anywhere from five to twenty yards for a first down, the Buckeye coverage fills the bill. Aside from putting the extra man in the short zones, the alignment effectively defends against screens with the defenders positioned to the outside and against draw plays with the extra inside linebacker. Short sprint-out passes, options, and reverses also are made impotent by the defense's alignment. The weakness of the two-deep coverage is exposed when three receivers are allowed to freely attack the two defensive backs' three-deep zones. Your defense must not let this occur.

Usually our defenses adjust to a "Buckeye" call by rotating the three defensive backs to the strong side of the offensive formation. This puts the strongside cornerback in a position tight to the line of scrimmage on the wide receiver's outside shoulder. His assignment from this position is to shiver, or harass, the wide receiver and force him to take an inside release on his ensuing pattern. After jamming the wide receiver, the cornerback is responsible for the flat pass zone on drop-back passes and for any action that comes wide to his side. If it were an option play, he would take the pitch man. The defensive back in the safety's position would rotate over and align on the strongside hash mark approximately ten yards deep. The weakside cornerback would align on the backside hash mark. These deep backs are responsible to cover all deep passes by retreating down the hash marks. Brutus (WOLB) aligns on the weakside wide receiver in a similar position as the strongside cornerback assumed. The rotation of the secondary allows the linebackers to slide toward the weakside. Maco (SOLB) aligns near the strongside hook zone, Nasty (ILB) in the middle zone, and Panther (IRLB) over the weakside hook zone.

The defensive player who assumes the middle position can be given "game-breaking" assignments. Since he is an extra defender, he can be set free to make the big play. He might be designated as your interception specialist or be assigned to cover one expected play or one great back. With practice, this middle defender can learn to set up the quarterback to throw the ball to a certain receiver. Many quarterbacks when dropping back to pass key the middle linebacker for coverage rotation. If the middle linebacker goes left, the quarterback throws right. If he goes right the quarterback throws left. Your middle man in the Buckeye coverage can purposely start to drop one way, set the quarterback up, and drive for the interception in the other direction. Because this coverage leaves only one linebacker inside, you would normally call a defensive line set that has one of the tackles in a position to protect an inside A gap. Many times you will use a "33" call with Buckeye coverage. Diagrams 5.9a, b, c, and d illustrate Buckeye coverage with different situations and alignments.

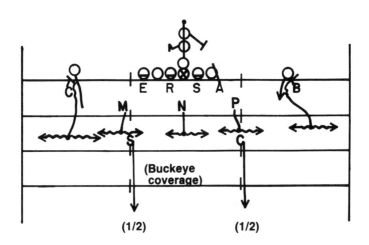

Diagram 5.9a   Buckeye coverage against a pro-set in the middle of the hash marks, with drop-back pass action. The defensive call is "33 Buckeye."

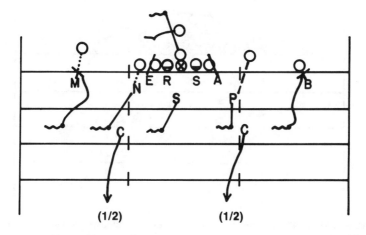

Diagram 5.9b   A Tight 33 Buckeye shows the safety playing the middle position and both outside linebackers aligned on the wide receivers. The middle position should be manned by one of your best athletes. The wide slot makes Panther (IRLB) move out toward the curl area.

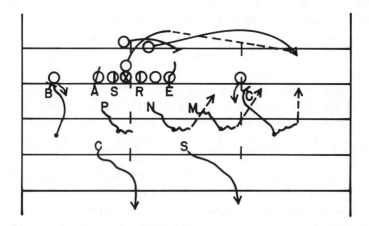

Diagram 5.9c   Buckeye coverage coupled with a "22" call. Starting from the hash mark, the two-deep backs adjust to the ball and to the sprint-out action of the quarterback.

"Kansas" (Man-to-Man) Coverage
With Linebacker Blitzes

Although the foundation of the Super Split System is successful application of the various zone defenses, at times you will want to "lock on"

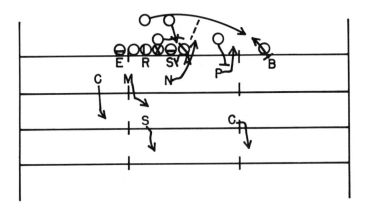

Diagram 5.9d   A 43 Buckeye against a tight-end-only side, with a wide-slot look to the other side. Your defense is in a great position to stop the offense's option.

man-to-man with the potential receivers. These situations are most apparent in the goal line area, where just the slightest separation of receiver from defender can result in a completed pass—or worse, a touchdown. The other situation arises when you want to blitz two or more of your linebackers. Taking two or more defenders out of a zone defense scheme leaves too many holes to be considered a sound move, without each defender being responsible for an assigned receiver.

The essential elements of a good, sound man-to-man defense are a reliable method that defines who covers whom and skilled individual technique. If your *Kansas* (Man-to-Man) coverage is called in conjunction with a blitz, it is important that your stunting linebackers get to the quarterback quickly. You can't expect your coverage people to stay with their man forever. Our system, which isolates for each defender the offensive receiver he is to cover, is explained in the section on the linebacker's assignments versus the drop-back pass (see Diagrams 3.41 and 3.42). This section will combine the defensive back's use of the system with the linebacker's. Also, our technique for Man-to-Man coverage is reviewed in the section dealing with the secondary's responsibilities and techniques (chapter 4, ''Man-to-Man Technique'').

To facilitate calling linebacker blitzes, the offensive line gaps have been given names to go with the letters assigned to the gaps (see Diagram c). Each linebacker who is called on to blitz communicates to the defensive lineman involved in the stunt which gap the linebacker will hit by calling out the name of that specific gap. The defensive lineman, in return, stunts to an opposite or corresponding gap. The two A and two B gaps are given differ-

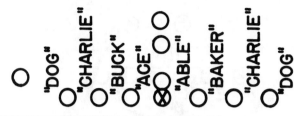

Diagram 5.10   In this basic offensive formation, the spaces inside and outside of each lineman have distinctive names beginning with the letter that corresponds to each particular gap.

ent names so that the inside linebackers can hit gaps on either side of the center without confusing the defensive linemen. Diagram 5.10 defines the offensive gap nomenclature for implementing the stunt package.

Inside Linebacker Blitz

When two or more linebackers are sent on a blitz, the remaining seven-spokes must know exactly which receivers to cover. For simplicity, we limit the linebacker blitz schemes in our system to just the inside line-backers or just the outside linebackers, or to a call that sends all four line-backers. To send the two inside linebackers (Nasty and Panther) on a blitz, a "Kansas" (telling the rest of the defense they are in Man-to-Man cover-age) *NiP* call would be made ("NiP" being derived from the first letters of Nasty and Panther). When the inside linebackers are sent on a blitz, the remaining spokes cover the #1 and #5 receivers with the cornerbacks, the #2 and #4 receivers with the outside linebackers, and the #3 receiver with the safety. If receiver #3 stays in the backfield and blocks, the safety is free to help cover deep zones or to double up on a particular receiver. You could also choose to send him on a delayed safety blitz after check-ing to see if #3 is being used for pass protection. Diagrams 5.11a and b show the inside linebackers calling their particular A or B gap on a Tight-44-Kansas-NiP.

The inside linebackers may choose (or be assigned) to blitz through the C gaps also. This is not common, but it may be effective versus certain offensive plays—the inside veer, for example. Because the C gap is quite a distance from his inside alignment, the linebacker may choose not to hit his called gap if the ball moves in the opposite direction. In other words, if the ball goes toward the gap he is to hit, he will execute the stunt; if it doesn't, he won't. Although the *Charlie* call is a good stunt from the

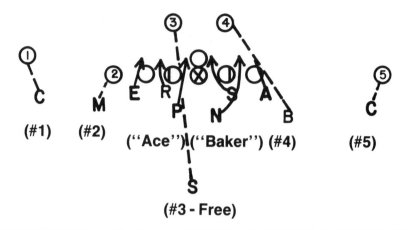

Diagram 5.11a   Although the cornerbacks are shown tight to the line of scrimmage, in open-field area they may choose to align deeper and use a loose Man-to-Man coverage. Nasty (ILB) is performing an ''Ace'' call and Panther (IRLB) a ''Baker'' call.

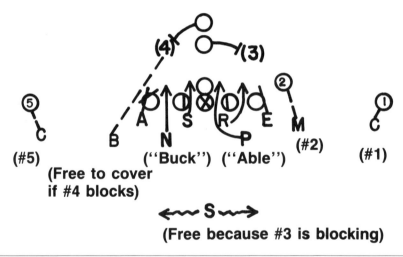

Diagram 5.11b   A Tight 22 set with a ''Kansas-NiP'' call against an offense strong to the defense's right side. Nasty (ILB) has called a ''Buck'' and Panther (IRLB) has called an ''Able.''

Tight alignments, it can also be called from the normal setup. Diagram 5.12 shows both inside linebackers using a Charlie stunt from a 42 set, with a ''Kansas-NiP'' call. Notice how the defensive ends hit different gaps if they are lined up in the base or the Tight position. The defensive end positioned over the tight end hits the D gap. The end aligned tight hits the B gap.

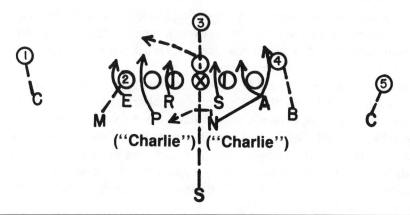

("Charlie") ("Charlie")

Diagram 5.12 The dotted lines show that Nasty (ILB) is not fulfilling his blitz assignment because the ball is moving in the opposite direction.

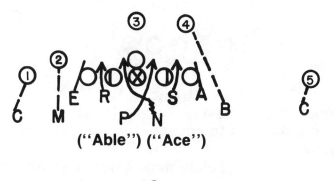

("Able") ("Ace")

S (#3 or Free)

Diagram 5.13 With a Tight 44 defense and a call of "Kansas-NiP," the stunt is for Nasty (ILB) to call an "Ace" and Panther (IRLB) to call an "Able."

Diagram 5.13 shows the inside linebackers utilizing the offensive gap nomenclature to perform a *cross* blitz. This blitz is made more effective if one of the inside linebackers cheats up a bit before hitting his gap.

Outside Linebacker Blitz

The call *MoBy* signifies to the defense that you want the outside linebackers to blitz. With a "MoBy" call, the cornerbacks still cover the #1 and #5 men, while the safety now covers the #2 man, and Panther (IRLB) adjusts his position to cover the #4 man. Nasty (ILB) stays inside and covers the #3 receiver if he goes out on a pass pattern. Remember, when any

of the receivers remain as pass protection blockers, the defender responsible is released to cover free. Your coverage men should always remember
the possibility that their man may fake pass block responsibilities and run
a delayed route. The outside linebackers' blitz routes are normally limited
to the outside gaps (C and D). Sometimes with a split end to their side
they will call a B gap blitz. The outside linebackers and defensive ends
must be aware that even when the offensive end splits out on their side,
two hypothetical "gaps" still remain outside the offensive tackle's position. This designation of gaps becomes important when you are stunting
all four linebackers so that there is a gap available for all four blitzing
defenders. Diagrams 5.14a and b illustrate the outside linebackers blitzing and the resulting coverage.

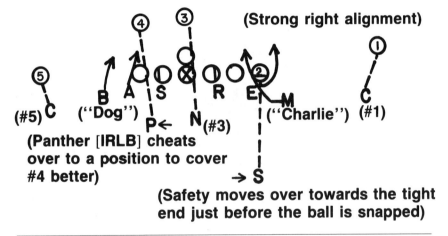

Diagram 5.14a In a base 44 set with a "Kansas-MoBy" call, Brutus (WOLB) has made
a "Dog" call, which sends him through an imaginary D gap as his defensive end hits
the C gap.

All-Four-Linebacker Blitz

When you really want to "sell the farm," you can send all of your linebackers on a blitz with a *Spike* call. When sending all eight front defenders,
there are some precautions. The inside linebackers should limit their rush
to the inside four gaps (two A and two B) and the outside linebackers should
limit their blitz route to either the C or the D gaps. Coaches are often
inhibited in calling an all-out blitz because of their (well-founded) fear
of the offense running a screen, draw, or quick-hitting trap play. An all-

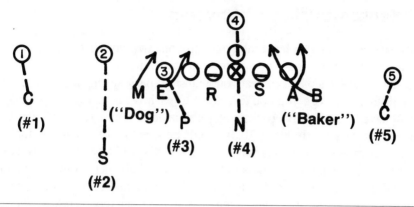

Diagram 5.14b   In a 33 "Kansas-MoBy" call against a Trips set, Nasty (ILB) stays inside with the #4 man and Panther (IRLB) moves outside to cover #3. Brutus (WOLB) has called "Baker."

out "Spike" call attempts to reduce that fear by delegating certain blitzers the responsibility of checking for these plays as they blitz.

Whichever defender's blitz route is through the D gap automatically looks for screen action forming to his side. If he reads screen action (offensive linemen or backs slipping to the outside), he pulls out of his blitz pattern and moves to the outside in the screen area. Whichever defender hits the Ace gap will attract a blocker or two, but he stays under control to check first for a quick inside trap, second, for a draw play. Diagram 5.15 demonstrates the all-out rush. Because there are only three defenders left to cover the receivers, the safety plays loose, reading the quarterback's eyes and being aware of the #2, #3, and #4 receivers.

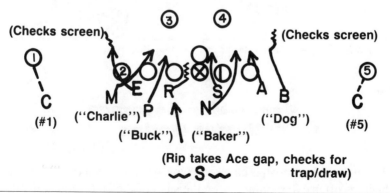

Diagram 5.15   A Tight 42 Kansas-Spike: "Checkers" are aware of their assignments.

"Kansas-Buckeye" Coverage

Kansas coverage can be combined with your two-deep/five-under Buckeye scheme. This would be an excellent "prevent" defense versus an opponent who feels they can beat you with short passes, screens, draws, etc. With this coverage you could lock on to each receiver man-to-man and still have two defensive backs covering the deep zones. If the #3 man did not enter the pattern, Nasty (ILB) would be free to blitz, roam, or double up on some receiver. Diagram 5.16 shows this coverage. Notice that the strong cornerback and Brutus (WOLB) cover their men from an outside position, similar to the position they take when in the Buckeye zone coverage. From this position they attempt to make their receivers take an inside route as they cover them man-to-man.

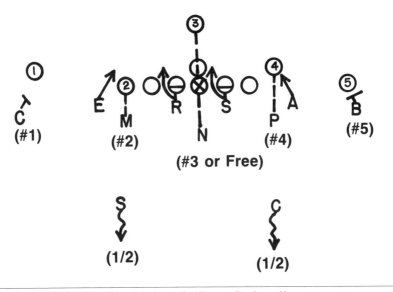

Diagram 5.16   A Wide 33, with the call "Kansas-Buckeye."

Man-to-Man Coverage
Versus Motion

When using Man-to-Man coverage, you need a set method to cover, or adjust to, offensive motion before the snap of the ball. Simplistically described, each defender goes with his man whenever he is in motion—we use this approach whenever possible. In goal line situations the "go-with-your-man" rule is in force. The only time our defenders "bump" their motion man to someone else is to allow Nasty (ILB) and the safety to remain in inside positions. Diagrams 5.17a and b demonstrate that when the defense has called for the inside linebackers to blitz with a "Kansas-NiP" call, everyone covering a receiver can go with his man when he goes in motion (except for the safety's man [#3]). Diagram 5.17b shows the safety bumping his man to other defenders when he goes in motion.

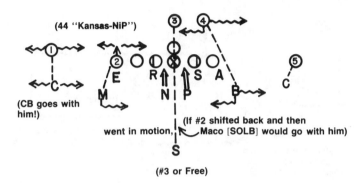

Diagram 5.17a The curved lines show each defender's man starting in motion and the defender going with him. The defender should stay with his man throughout the motion distance.

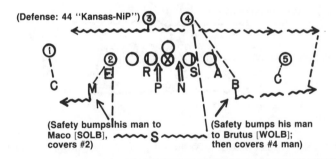

Diagram 5.17b When the #3 receiver (the safety's man) goes in motion to either side, the safety bumps his man to the outside linebackers and then covers their man.

If the defense has called for an outside linebacker blitz (MoBy), the only players the safety will bump his #2 receiver to are the cornerbacks. If the #2 receiver goes in motion past one of the outside receivers, the safety can bump his man to the cornerback and then cover the cornerback's man. As mentioned, we also like to keep Nasty (ILB) inside most of the time (this would not be true if both inside linebackers were similar in ability). If there were two remaining backs in the backfield and Nasty's #3 back happened to go in motion, Panther (IRLB) would switch men and go with the motion man, and Nasty would cover the remaining back. The only time Nasty could be run out of the middle is if the offense utilized a rare formation with all backs removed to flanker positions. Diagram 5.18a shows the safety bumping his man to the cornerbacks on a "Kansas-MoBy" call. Diagram 5.18b shows Panther picking up Nasty's man when he goes in motion.

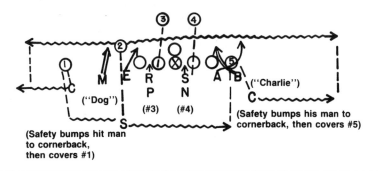

Diagram 5.18a   With an 11 Stack defense and a call of "Kansas-MoBy," the safety bumps his man to the cornerbacks so that he can stay in the deeper middle position.

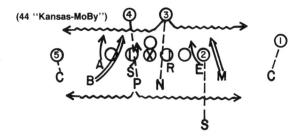

Diagram 5.18b   Panther (IRLB) picks up Nasty's (ILB) man no matter which direction he goes in motion. Nasty covers the remaining back.

Chapter 6

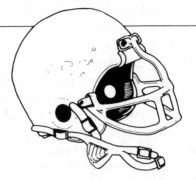

Adjusting the Split for Goal Line Use

Goal line and short yardage situations necessitate a major change in the philosophy or standard approach to defensive play that has been accepted with the base split-four defense. No longer does the "bend, but do not break" design prove applicable. Your defense has to attack. They have to put defensive emphasis on one phase of the offense's game.

22 "Kansas" Goal Line Defense

The 22 *Kansas* goal line defense communicates to its opponents, "If you want a chance to score, you had better pass the ball, because you're not going to score on the ground." To back this up, the defense aggressively attacks the offense's running game, preventing the offense from "owning" the line of scrimmage, and goes for the big negative-yardage, defensive play. Because of the defense's goal line strategy, certain plays, such as quick traps, and passes become more of a threat than when the defense was operating more conservatively. The key to successful goal line defense is to nullify these plays through play awareness and aggressive pressure, while attacking the #1 threat—the power runs.

Although the defensive philosophy is altered in goal line situations, the front-eight/three-deep scheme fits conveniently and effectively with the aggressive goal line attack. Remember that the front-eight in the base defense are designated run-stoppers. They are the same in goal line defense, only much more aggressive. They concern themselves with causing offensive breakdowns, rather than taking the more passive read-and-react approach. The three-deep defensive backs make the biggest adjustment, turning from a cool "Dr. Jekyll," covering his man with intelligent zone principles, to a mean "Mr. Hyde," using hard-nosed Man-to-Man coverage techniques.

The alteration of the base defense into goal line alignments begins with the inversion of the defensive ends and tackles. The ends move inside and align themselves in a #2 position over the offensive guard's inside knee. The defensive tackles move out to a #3 alignment over the offensive tackles. The purpose of this switch is evident. You want your quicker defensive ends occupying the inside gaps, where defensive penetration is a must. The bigger, stronger defensive tackles are placed over the offense's bigger men, which makes for a more equal match.

With a goal line call, the defensive ends' #2 alignment and stance require major adjustment. They align as tight to the line of scrimmage as possible, in a very low four-point stance. Their outside shoulder must cover the offensive guard's inside knee. This means that the defensive end's outside foot is just inside the offensive guard's inside foot. In the goal line stance, the defensive ends' elbows are bent at a 90° angle, their chins are about nine inches from the ground, and their legs are up under their bodies to provide maximum extension. They must keep their heads up, "bulling" their necks, to be able to see the ball being snapped—which signals their movement. On movement, the defensive ends will explode through the inside knee of the offensive guard. To force your defensive ends to stay low, teach them to hit their bellies on the ground as they penetrate into the backfield. As they penetrate, they are responsible for their gap, and they will attempt to grab the quarterback's near leg as they move forward. Your penetrating ends will hit their bellies, but only for a moment, as they attempt to surge into the opponent's backfield and disrupt the play.

Emphasize to your defensive ends the two major reasons for aligning on the guard's inside knee. The first is to force the offensive guard to block the defensive end if the ball is being run to that side of the center. You do not want the offense to be able to scoop-block the defensive ends with the center, which allows the guard to block your inside linebackers. The second result you need from your penetrating defensive ends is, if they stay underneath the offensive guard's block, to create a lane for their inside linebackers to attack through in the B gap area. If the defensive ends fail to stay beneath the blocker's shoulder pads, they stand the risk of getting "run back," which walls off your inside linebackers and basically nullifies the strength of your goal line defense's alignment. Diagrams 6.1a, b, and c illustrate some of these tenets of defensive ends' goal line play.

Diagram 6.1a The defensive ends' exaggerated goal line stance facilitates their assignment of low penetration.

Diagram 6.1b Foot placement and the direction of the defensive ends' charge into the backfield.

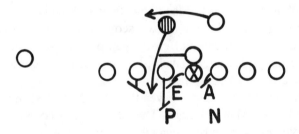

Diagram 6.1c The offense scoop-blocks the defensive end, allowing the offensive guard to block the linebacker. This is a big defensive mistake.

Rip (SDT) and Stud (WDT) align in a #3 position, tight to the line of scrimmage on the offensive tackle. They use their normal three-point stance, but place more weight on their support arm. The defensive tackles' goal line duty calls for them to nullify the tackle's block, preferably on the offensive side of the line of scrimmage. They use their normal tripod or flipper technique combined with a more forceful forward extension. If there is a tight end aligned to the tackle's outside, the defensive tackle is responsible for defeating the tackle's block and protecting the C gap. Versus a double-team block, he must not get driven back and wall off his linebackers.

If there is no tight end to the outside, the defensive tackle is responsible for the gap to his inside (B gap) after defeating the tackle's block. Rip (SDT) and Stud (WDT) must reasonably maintain their line of scrimmage leverage, or the defense will be unable to successfully defend its flanks. With the defensive ends effectively penetrating into the middle gaps and the defensive tackles solidly encamped in the off-tackle area, you have the makings of a successful goal line stand.

In goal line defense, the outside linebackers do not have pass coverage responsibilities, but instead join the four-down and aggressively rush the ball. Maco (SOLB) and Brutus (WOLB) line up tight to the line of scrimmage, in a two-point stance one yard outside of the tight end (or offensive tackle versus the split end side). They key the snap of the ball for movement and drive hard to the hip of the near-back. Their assignment includes taking the pitch-back out on the option play and turning sweeps, pitch-outs, bootlegs, and roll-outs to the inside, while looking for misdirection plays when the ball starts away.

Nasty (ILB) and Panther (IRLB) line up in a tight stack behind the defensive ends. They are responsible for the #3 and #4 receivers, but first must stop straight-ahead runs aimed at the inside gaps. Versus a drop-back pass where both remaining backs stay and block, at least one of the inside linebackers will blitz the passer. Also, their stack position is not a rigid placement; they will cheat to the side of scouted tendencies and coverage responsibilities, and threaten offensive gap penetration. The inside linebackers normally play aggressively, but in goal line defense they really go for broke.

The cornerbacks and safety cover the #1, #2, and #5 receivers with aggressive Man-to-Man technique. The safety usually covers the tight end, but it is relatively simple to exchange assignments with a cornerback or outside linebacker so that the strongest athlete covers the tight end. The defender who covers the tight end should align right in his face and attempt to defeat his block. When the tight end blocks to the inside, the defender must shut down the off-tackle play by moving inside, taking the lead blocker on with his inside shoulder, and jamming the play inside. Versus the outside veer play (a good goal line play), the defender would tackle the dive-back. When the tight end does release on a pass, his defender forcefully inhibits his pattern action and timing and attempts to maintain a position between the ball and his man.

Goal Line Defense Versus Selected Offensive Plays

Goal line defenses are confronted by many ''must-stop'' plays and plays designed to defeat man-to-man, penetrating defensive attacks. The following diagrams highlight some of these plays along with some common adjustments and calls that can be used to modify the basic 22 Kansas goal line defense.

''Must-Stop'' Plays

The *isolation play,* the *halfback dive,* and the quick-hitting *off-tackle play* are three plays that would be considered ''must-stop'' ones by any goal line defense. Diagrams 6.2a, b, and c demonstrate the actions taken by the goal line defenders from the 22 invert alignment.

The Isolation Play

Many times the *isolation play* is run with wedge blocking, with the tailback attempting to leap up and over the line. In these cases the defensive end's penetration and the defensive tackle's control of the line of scrimmage are vital to the success of the defense. The linebackers cannot have linemen in their faces when they have to leap up over the pile and stuff the runner.

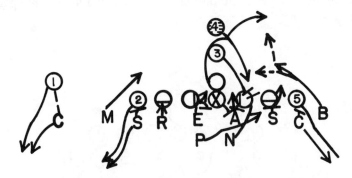

Diagram 6.2a   The isolation play will defeat a linebacker who reacts too slowly. The inside linebacker must expect this play and meet the blocker on the other side of the line of scrimmage. The first linebacker to the play should cut the lead blocker down, which allows pursuit to tackle the ball carrier.

The Halfback Dive

In the *halfback dive,* Rip (SDT) delivers his defensive blow and takes C gap responsibilities. This leaves the B gap for the inside linebacker's aggressive scrape attack.

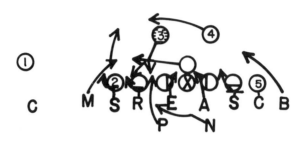

Diagram 6.2b   The halfback dive is a quick hitting, base blocking play that allows the halfback to find a crack in the line and slip through for a score. The defense must hold the line of scrimmage AND fill the gaps.

The Off-Tackle Play

Versus the Power-"I" *off-tackle play,* your goal line defense has five or more defenders in the immediate area. Maco (SOLB) squeezes the running lane down so that the tailback cannot bump to the outside when the C gap closes up. Versus the double-team block, the goal line inside linebacker can usually penetrate through the B gap and disrupt the play before it gets to the line of scrimmage.

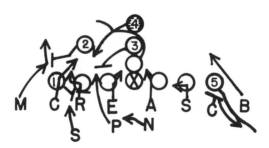

Diagram 6.2c   The off-tackle play is a power move that requires defensive strength-with-numbers to be defeated.

Four Tough Options to Stop

Unless the offense sneaks a quick-hitting inside trap play or has an excellent corner fade passing scheme, probably the most difficult plays you will have to defend on the goal line are the option plays. The first thing the offense will try with an option series is to run off your Man-to-Man coverage personnel. This usually leaves you with just eight players to cover all three potential ball carriers (to just one side of the center you only have four defenders plus pursuit to defend the three possible options). When opposing well-coached option teams, we have chosen a loose Man-to-Man coverage on the wide receivers when in goal line defense. This enables the defensive backs to jump on the option when they see it develop. Diagrams 6.3a, b, c, and d show the goal line defense versus four of the toughest options to stop in football.

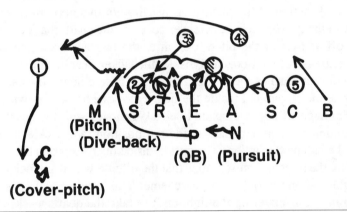

Diagram 6.3a   The outside veer is a dynamite goal line play that will test all of your onside defenders. It uses quick hitting with straight-ahead blocking and can be very deceptive.

Versus the Outside Veer

For your defense to have a chance at stopping the *outside veer,* they must keep from getting driven back off the line of scrimmage. Penetration, starting with the defensive ends' A gap assignment, goes a long way toward the play's defeat. When the tight end blocks inside, the safety is released to aggressively move inside and attack the first offensive back he comes to (versus the sprint option this would be the quarterback). Now the onside linebackers must succeed in defeating their portion of the option. The outside linebacker is responsible for the pitch, but instead of going right to the pitch-back, the good outside backer will pull up under control when he recognizes the outside veer. He should use the skate technique (described in the linebacker technique section) to deny the quarterback an unobstructed running lane, but still enable the defender to cover the pitch-back.

It is important that your defense understand the relative threat each running back poses on an option play. With the outside veer, the dive-back is the man the offense wants to carry the ball. Consequently, he is the man you must stop first. If you stuff him, you force the quarterback to carry the ball. With the outside veer, the quarterback is the second most dangerous man with the ball, because of his advantageous position when he pulls the ball from the dive-back. If not attacked immediately, he can slip directly into the end zone. The pitch is normally a last resort with the outside veer. Because of the pitch-back's presnap alignment and the fast outside action of the play, he is usually not in a good pitch relationship with the quarterback. A defender covering the quarterback can usually come off and cover the pitch-back after the ball has been pitched.

An aggressive, well-coached inside linebacker may be able to stop the play before it reaches the corner. Often the onside-inside linebacker can penetrate the B gap and tackle the quarterback as he goes down the line of scrimmage. If not, the inside linebacker moves with the quarterback, maintaining the one-half man inside-out position, and tackles him if he keeps the ball on the option. The onside-inside linebacker and the defender covering the tight end must realize that the offense will also block out with the tight end on the outside veer scheme. This would require the safety (assuming he is covering the tight end) to take the quarterback, and the defensive tackle and the inside linebacker would have the dive-back. The backside-inside linebacker must use all of his speed and energy to back up the onside defender's attempt to squelch the outside veer. The backside linebacker is especially concerned with a possible cut-back by the dive-back.

Versus the Inside Veer

A major difference between the outside veer and the *inside veer* is that the pitch-back (especially a fast one) is much more of a threat with the inside veer. The outside linebacker knows this and goes directly to the pitch-back to take him out of the play. The defensive tackle has to shut down the fullback when his offensive tackle goes inside and keep the tackle off of his inside linebacker. The onside-inside linebacker, similar to his duty

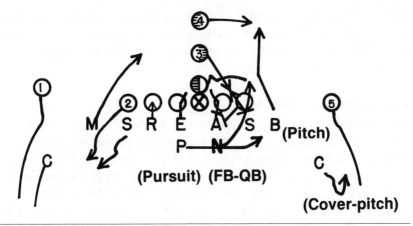

Diagram 6.3b   The well-run inside veer can also cause problems for your goal line defense. Again, defensive pressure coupled with strong discipline is key in defeating this play.

versus the outside veer, takes the quarterback from an inside-out position. This play can also be made more complicated if the offense sometimes blocks out on the defensive tackle, allowing the back to escape inside. The defensive tackle is responsible for this gap when the end is split to his side, but the inside linebacker still has to be there if the back breaks through. The backside-inside linebacker again has to pursue like ''h---!''

Versus the Full House–Wishbone

The *full house–wishbone* formation allows the safety to attack the quarterback because Maco (SOLB) denies the pitch-back *and* his blocker from

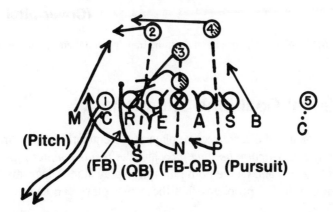

Diagram 6.3c   The goal line defense against the inside veer action from the full house–wishbone look.

getting into the play. Rip (SDT) shuts the fullback down, and Nasty (ILB) assists with the fullback while working out to the quarterback if he keeps the ball. Panther (IRLB) pursues quickly to protect against any defensive breakdowns or a play action pass.

Versus the Trap Option

The *trap* option takes your backside-inside linebacker out of the play with the trap fake and usually gets pretty good blocking position on your defensive tackle with the pulling guard. The play appears to be an inside trap, so the defensive tackle shuts down laterally, leaving himself vulnerable to the guard's "log" block. This leaves the outside linebacker and the onside-inside linebacker to stop the play. The backside-inside linebacker can usually come off the trap fake and get into the play.

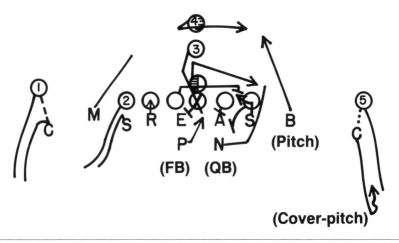

Diagram 6.3d   When effectively executed, the trap option presents problems unique to what most defenses usually see.

Additional Goal Line Situations

Two additional and often effective plays run frequently in goal line situations are the *play-action bootleg pass* and the *inside counter play,* where the offside guard and tackle both pull to the play side. Diagrams 6.4 and 6.5 demonstrate the problems that these two plays can cause.

Versus the Play-Action Bootleg Pass

As you can see, the two primary defenders of the play-action bootleg pass are the weakside-outside linebacker Brutus and the safety, who must cover the tight end across the field. If the safety does his job well, he makes it so difficult for the tight end to release that he then is not in the proper position to have the ball thrown to him. Nasty (ILB), after seeing the actual direction of the play, aggressively attacks the passer if he has any chance of getting to him. Panther (IRLB) quickly tries to get back into the short passing zones after he realizes that it is a bootleg pass.

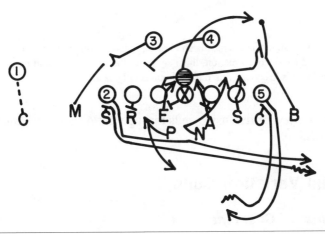

Diagram 6.4 With your outside linebacker aggressively attacking the near-back's outside hip, you are in a much better position than most defenses versus the bootleg pass. If your outside linebacker is aware of the pulling guard, he will not get blocked out or allow the quarterback to escape up inside.

Versus the Inside Counter Play

To defeat the inside counter play, your defense must first work against it in practice. The outside linebackers are coached to alter their normal angle of penetration. They must be taught to expect the play to be an inside counter if the ball starts away. The near slotback often starts in motion prior to the snap of the ball. This key tells the outside linebacker (Maco) to penetrate down the line of scrimmage with his initial charge the same as if the play action started to the other side. When the inside counter does come to his side, the outside linebacker has to take the lead blocker (usually the pulling guard) out with a low "block" that creates a pile-up in the area where the play is to be run. This tactic usually ends up taking the pulling tackle out of the play as well. The slotback, whose interference is lying on the ground in the backfield, becomes easy prey for the defensive tackle and linebacker pursuit. Even though Nasty's (ILB) fullback key initially takes him away from the point of attack, by reading the pulling guard's action he can quickly adjust and move to the ball. Excellent

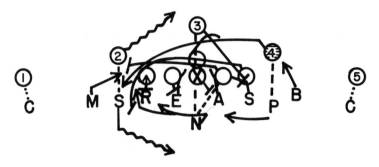

Diagram 6.5   The inside counter is another play that can be a thorn in the side. When run from the double-slot formation, this play is not the typical slow-hitting counter play. Even with the misdirection, this play hits amazingly fast.

penetration by your defensive ends through the A gaps will usually spoil the play as well.

Special Variation Calls

22 "Kansas" Goal Line "Gap"

A *Gap* call added to the normal goal line call sends the defensive tackles blitzing through the B gaps. The "Gap" call is used in situations where you are confident that the offense will run a quarterback or fullback sneak into the middle of the line. Diagram 6.6 shows the defense's reactions to the belly option with a "Gap" call.

22 "Kansas" Goal Line "Slam"

When you decide to totally go for broke and to anticipate that the offense will not pass or run outside, you might call for the *Slam*. This call sends

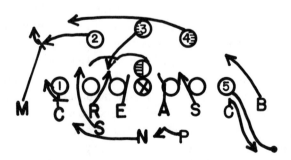

Diagram 6.6   The 22 Kansas Goal Line *Gap* against the belly option.

all of your front men into the inside gaps. The inside linebackers are still responsible for #3 and #4 receivers, but they are up and ready to protect against the inside run. If there is a wide receiver, the cornerbacks take themselves out of the blitz and go out and cover their man. Diagram 6.7 demonstrates this call versus the tailback *Alley-oop* play.

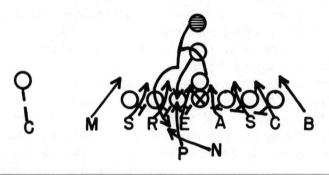

Diagram 6.7 The 22 Kansas Goal Line *Slam*.

"Tarzan" Goal Line Defense Versus the Extra Point or Field Goal

The 22 Kansas goal line can be adjusted very easily into an overload formation that will create a better opportunity for your defense to block the opponent's extra point or field goal try. This defense is usually called 22 Kansas Goal Line–*Tarzan* to remind the defense to initially align in the goal line look in case the opponents come out in a "running" formation. Once the opponent has shown (by alignment) the intention to kick, the defense will shift over into the Tarzan look. Tarzan may be called to the left or the right, but typically is run from the left adjustment. Diagram 6.8 shows the goal line defense adjusted into the Tarzan look.

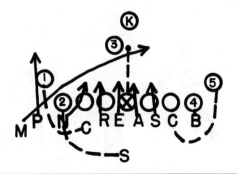

Diagram 6.8 The 22 Kansas Goal Line–*Tarzan*.

With a "Tarzan" call, the four defensive linemen squeeze in as tight as they can to the ball so that all four are covering just three offensive linemen. On the snap they attempt to drive the three blockers back to the ball. At the last moment they raise their arms to try to deflect the kick. The cornerbacks come in and align in a three-point stance in the face of the offensive tackles—they want the tackles to try to block them. As the ball is being snapped, the cornerbacks quickly sprint out and get in a position where they can cover their man in case of a fake.

The safety aligns in the middle over the center and threatens to rush; when the ball is snapped he rushes out to cover the tight end. Three of the linebackers are directly involved in blocking the kick, while Brutus (WOLB) covers the weakside tight end man-to-man. Nasty (ILB) aligns right in front of the tight end. On the snap of the ball he rushes hard to the inside, making the tight end move inside to block him. This is very important, because it helps open up the lane for the main kick-blocker, "Tarzan." Panther (IRLB) aligns tight on the line of scrimmage and rushes through the up-back's outside shoulder. He wants to draw the up-back to the outside also to help open up the blocker's lane. Maco (SOLB), who is playing Tarzan, lines up just outside of Panther and just a mite deeper. On the snap of the ball he rushes the lane that has been made for him and attempts to block the kick. Any player on your team can play the part of Tarzan, if he has excellent speed and quickness and is willing to fling his body through the air.

"Tarzan–Bananas"

At the call of *Tarzan–Bananas,* everybody rushes the kick and you take the chance of the fake. Just the name of this defense seems to get the kids excited enough to go and block the kick. Diagram 6.9 illustrates this all-out attempt.

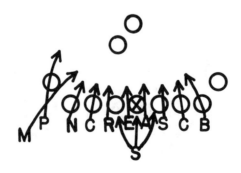

Diagram 6.9   "Tarzan-Bananas."

Chapter 7

The "Split" Punt Defense

Winning football coaches never underestimate the importance or value of a sound kicking game to a consistent, winning program. Although coaches sometimes mistakenly relate "the kicking game" to just the offensive side of the ball, most understand that a sound, solid defensive kicking game may be just as important to a winning team's attack.

Punt defense includes the punt rushes and the punt return. With many offenses electing to eliminate the huddle before lining up to punt, it is very important for your defense to adjust quickly and simply into, or out of, their punt defense alignment. The *Split* punt alignment is very similar to the base 44 alignment. Assuming that you use the same personnel for your punt defense and your regular defense, you can make the adjustment from one to the other very readily. By signaling in your defensive punt scheme from the sideline, your defense can be waiting for their call from the base 44 positions before adjusting to the call. This enables your defense to be prepared for an offense that runs their punt team onto the field as soon as the third-down play is over. If they come out in a running formation, your defense is ready. If they come out and line up in punt formation, again your team is able to quickly adjust.

When punt defense is called, your defensive players align in relatively the same position every time. There are, of course, adjustments to the various punt formations and situations where you might make a slight change to take advantage of an opponent's apparent weakness. The normal punt defense alignment puts your defensive tackles in a #4 alignment on the second man out from the center. The defensive ends align in a #3 position on the tight end (or tight slotback). If there is no tight end or slotback, the defensive ends move into a #4 alignment on the offensive tackle.

The inside linebackers align in a #3 position on the first man from the center, who may be an up-back or a guard. The outside linebackers align one yard outside of the tight end (or tight slotback) in a position free from any immediate blockers. The cornerbacks again occupy the position over the offensive tackle (the third man out from the center in the standard punt formation). If there is a wide receiver in the offense's punt formation, the cornerback goes out to his normal coverage position. When in punt defense versus the standard punt formation, all of the front-ten defenders are tight to the line of scrimmage in a three-point stance that makes them appear as if they are going to rush the punt. The outside linebackers may use a two-point stance with the inside foot up if they feel they get a better view of the punter and their rush lane. A punt defense call includes an automatic Omaha coverage, and usually the safety is the defensive back who drops back to field the punt. Diagrams 7.1a, b, c, d, and e illustrate the Split punt defense alignments versus some of the most common punt formations.

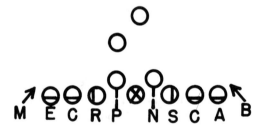

Diagram 7.1a Punt defense alignment against the standard spread punt alignment.

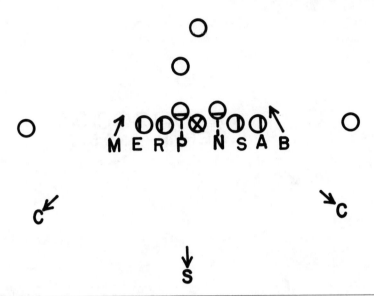

Diagram 7.1b Defensive punt alignment against the spread punt formation with split ends.

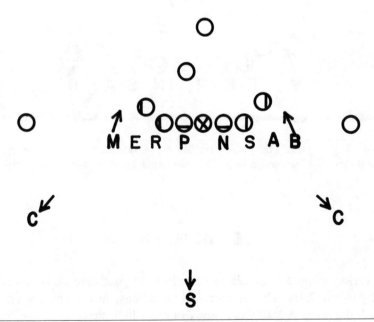

Diagram 7.1c Punt defense against the double-slot, or run-and-shoot, punt formation.

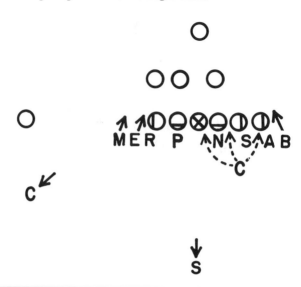

Diagram 7.1d   Versus the full house punt formation, a cornerback is freed up to threaten a gap if he does not have a wide receiver to his side.

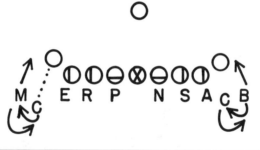

Diagram 7.1e   Against a tight-punt formation, the outside linebackers rush through the D gap if there is a big enough split. They can switch positions with the cornerbacks.

Punt Rush

The variety of punt rush schemes available to your defense is described mostly by numbers. The numbers tell the defense how many players are to rush the punt. A "10" call, for example, indicates that all ten front-line defenders are to rush. The most common punt rushes send eight, six, five, or four of the front-line defenders after the punt block. Basically, the more men you rush, the better chance you have of blocking the punt, but, conversely, the offense has a better chance of succeeding with a fake punt.

A "10" call, therefore, would normally mean that you are desperate and willing to take a chance. A "4" call, on the other hand, shows a desire to rush the punt, but very cautiously. Whenever the defenders are not part of the punt rush attack, they first drop back, covering their zones, and then lock on and block the closest punt-coverage man in their area. They will run with him from an inside-out position, attempting to wall him off from the punt returner.

The cornerbacks often find themselves aligned in a position to cover their outside third zone, because the punt team has deployed a wide receiver in its punt formation alignment. Although the cornerback is covering under zone rules, he is well aware that he must cover his wide-out very closely in case of the fake punt-and-pass play. Once the play is recognized as a punt, the cornerback locks on to his wide receiver in an inside-out or an outside-in position, whichever is made most available by the receiver's route to the punt returner. The wide receiver who goes straight for the punt returner can usually be blocked more readily to the inside, while the receiver who is told to contain the punt returner can usually be run to the outside.

"Big 8"

The "8" call (or the *Big 8*, as it is usually known) is the most common of the punt rush calls. On any punt rush call that includes them, the outside linebackers are the primary "designated" punt blockers. If your outside linebackers are not quick or courageous enough to perform this duty, you might consider substituting a special-team player or two for these important positions. The outside linebackers attack in a straight line at an angle that puts them at a spot four yards in front of the punter's presnap position. The outside linebackers do not run into each other because the punting team's "personal protector" will step up to block one or the other. Because of the "8" call, the cornerbacks pull out of their alignment over the tackles at the last moment and move back and out to cover their deep third zone. With the normal rush, the remainder of the front line rushes through the gap to their inside. This is why we have chosen the #4 alignment for the defensive tackles as their basic punt alignment. When the offensive blocker steps toward the outside to block the defensive tackle on his outside shoulder, it creates a larger lane to the inside. The defensive tackles can quickly cut to the inside and take advantage of this. Diagram 7.2 illustrates the basic Big 8 punt rush.

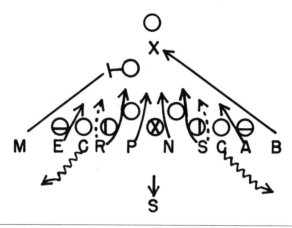

Diagram 7.2 The Big 8 punt rush.

The "8" call in Diagram 7.2 would be a "10" call if the cornerbacks were to rush their inside gap. There are some common moves or "deals" that can be added to the inside rush that may add to its effectiveness. The *Able* (or *Ace*), *Baker* (or *Buck*), and *Jam* calls are frequently used. You may let the inside four rushers call these moves themselves, with the inside linebackers making the decision. Also, on a normal rush such as shown in Diagram 7.2, you may choose to give your defensive tackle the ability to hit either side of the man he is aligned on, rather than just the inside gap. This charge is shown in dotted lines in Diagram 7.2. Diagrams 7.3a and b show the use of these deals with the inside four punt rushers.

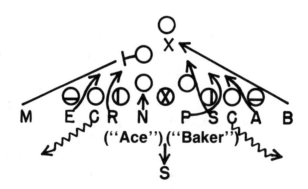

Diagram 7.3a In the Big 8 punt rush, Nasty (ILB) performs an Ace move with his defensive tackle and Panther (IRLB) calls a Baker stunt with his tackle.

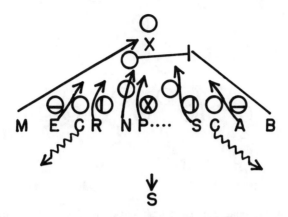

Diagram 7.3b A "Jam" call is being used to the left. The inside linebackers slide around from positions over the center to over the up-back. These two linebackers often make deals (e.g., cross-charges) between themselves stemming from the Jam setup. Nasty (ILB) has called "Ace" to keep his defensive tackle to the outside.

"6" Punt Rush

In a "6" call, the only thing that changes from the "8" call is that your inside linebackers pull out of the rush and cover the hook-to-curl zone before protecting the punt returner (Diagram 7.4). See Diagram 7.5 for "4" punt rush.

Diagram 7.6 illustrates a 5 punt rush with Kansas or Man-to-Man coverage. This covers all of the possible receivers with tight man coverage technique,

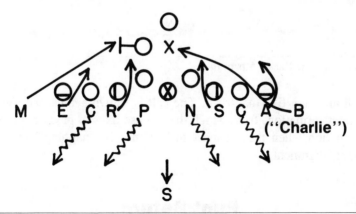

Diagram 7.4 In a "6" punt rush, Brutus (WOLB) has made a "Charlie" call with his defensive end.

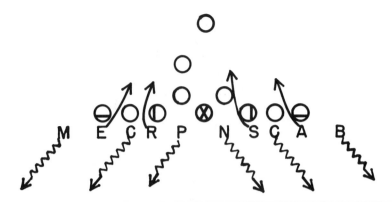

Diagram 7.5   A "4" punt rush may pull all four linebackers to protect their zones and then block for the punt returner. Rip (SDT) rushes his outside gap while Stud (WDT) chooses to rush the inside gap.

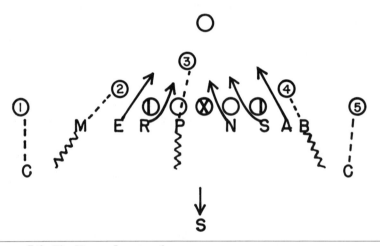

Diagram 7.6   The Kansas-5 punt rush.

but still allows a five-man rush. The call is shown against the run-and-shoot punt formation, from which the offense likes to pass or run out of the formation when they suspect the defense is "napping" or has an improper alignment.

Punt Return

We have chosen to keep the punt return as simple and limited as possible while remaining effective. Excellent blocking technique coupled with excellent running skills are more important to punt return success than is the design.

The punt return can be called to the left or to the right. The defensive alignment is exactly the same for the punt return as for the punt rush. Since the punt return only rushes one man (to force the punt), the number *1* signals the defense to run the punt return. *Blue* signifies a left return and *Red* a right return. The cornerbacks again release from their position in front of the offensive tackle just prior to the snap. They are responsible to get into an inside-out position with the offensive ends and to run with them down the field, walling them off from the inside. If the cornerbacks are aligned wide because of the punt formation, they still attempt to run their man out, but if he is determined to go inside straight to the returner, then the cornerbacks must force him inside with outside-in leverage.

Assuming you are running the punt return to your team's right side, the left outside linebacker would be the lone man rushing, forcing the punter to kick. After forcing the punt, he comes back toward the return and gets into position to escort the returner with a touchdown-saving last block. The right outside linebacker drops back on the snap of the ball and quickly moves inside, picking up the offensive center as he covers downfield. He wants to get into a position to wall the center off from the right side. It

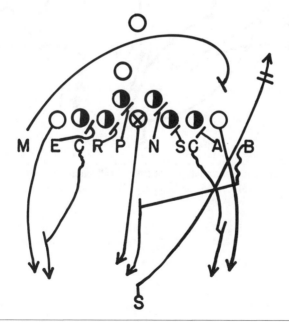

Diagram 7.7 A punt return right with a call of "1 Red."

is a passive type of block. The remaining six-down defenders hustle to a position shading the right side of the man they are over (the defensive ends will get position on the offensive man to their inside). It is the job of these defenders to stay locked on to their man from the position on the right side as they move down the field in the direction of the punt. This is not easy, but tenacity and desire sometimes get the job done where skill alone may fail. Diagram 7.7 demonstrates a punt return right.

Notice in Diagram 7.8 how the right cornerback hustled to a position that forces the wide receiver to be on the outside. This keeps the backside "hard-pressure" coverage man from making the tackle from the punt returner's blind side.

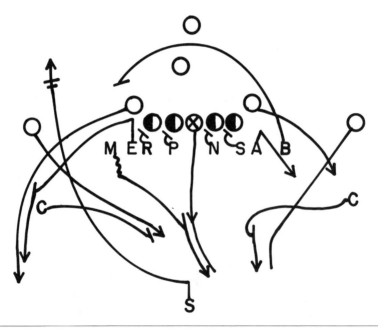

Diagram 7.8 The punt return left, or "1 Blue," call against a punt formation with two wide receivers. Evil (SDE) ends up blocking his man out, while the left cornerback is forced to drive his man inside.

Chapter 8

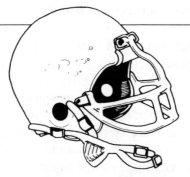

Getting the Ball Back With the Kamikaze Kickoff

The kickoff is one element of the game of football that appears very similar for almost any team at any level, from professional down through high school: Line the ball up in the middle of the field; kick it as far as you can, putting five of your wildest on one side and five on the other; stay in your lanes and get to the ball. This approach can be sound, especially if you have a kicker like most pro and college teams, who can boot the ball into or out of the end zone the majority of the time. But a problem arises when you don't have that great kicker who can consistently send the ball to the ten-yard line or better. Often the ball is kicked between the thirty-five and twenty-yard lines, usually floating at perfect height for the returner. This creates the opportunity for the receiving team to make a big game-breaking return.

The "Kamikaze" Kickoff

The *Kamikaze* kickoff was concocted by my coaching staff in 1971 in response to an article in a national coaching magazine stating that the average high school kickoff return reaches the returning team's forty-yard line.

This was a statistic that someone had compiled by charting hundreds of high school kickoff returns, and it seemed logical when you averaged in the very long returns. Our staff felt that if the other team would usually return our kickoff to the forty-yard line anyway, we might as well develop a kickoff system that gives us a chance to get the ball and reduces the chances of the opponent's returning a kickoff all the way, a devastating blow to any team's chance of winning. By "stealing" ideas from one coach here and another coach there, we came up with a kickoff (modified throughout the years) that has been very successful in what we set out to attain.

Since 1971, the Kamikaze kickoff has been used more than 500 times. The onside kick has been called approximately 70 percent of those times and has averaged over 25 percent (more than 100) ball recoveries. Only one onside kick was returned past our forty-yard line, and that was for a touchdown. It was, as are most big returns, a drastic breakdown in our coverage technique.

The Kamikaze kickoff is an audible kickoff. You can kick to six basic areas (shown in Diagram 8.1) when set and ready to kick the ball. Area 3 is our most often called area. The kicker's target is between the opponent's thirty-five and forty-yard lines on the far side of the field from the hash mark where the ball is placed (the ball is placed on the left hash mark at the forty-yard line). It is a good idea to come out in pregame and locate some object on the far side of the field from both forty-yard-line left hash marks with which the kicker can line up his kick to get the ball in that thirty-five to forty-yard-line target area. The target object might be a light pole, a bleacher pole, a tree—anything clearly visible directly behind the area where the kick is being aimed.

The kicker and coverage team line up as shown in Diagram 8.1. Each member of the kickoff team (other than the kicker) is identified by a number, as are the front-five members of the receiving team.

All kickoff calls are designed so that certain players are assigned specific duties that remain similar regardless of the call. Some players will be assigned to go for the ball, while others will be assigned to block or contain. You would like the most aggressive, "hungry" athletes to be the ball getters and the most disciplined to be the blockers and contain-men. The two widest are the fastest because they will be either the main ballmen or the safety on most calls.

The audible call is disguised simply by using a double-digit number. Before the game you decide whether to use the first or second digit as the indicator. For example, if you choose to kick to the 3 area and are using the second digit, the kicker could call "43," "13," etc. If you were using the first digit, you could call "34," "31," and so on.

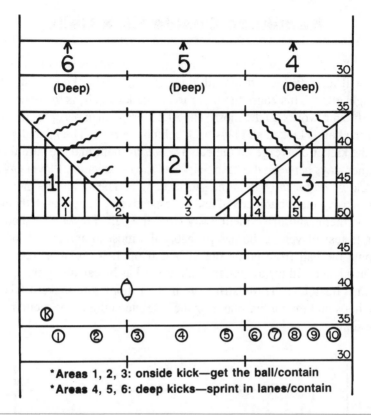

Diagram 8.1   The six basic areas to which the ball can be kicked along with the kickoff team's alignment and designated numbers. Note the front-five members of the return team and their corresponding numbers.

The kicker and coverage men are in the same alignment for all calls. The kicker must be in front of the rest of his team because his signal tells them when to start. He usually aligns about four yards from the ball, toward the left sideline. After making his audible call and checking to see that his teammates are ready, he drops his hand to signal the approach to the ball. The coverage men line up at a depth that puts them approximately one yard behind the ball when it is kicked. Since the coverage men have different speed abilities, they line up in various depths from the ball, usually between the thirty-three- and thirty-five-yard lines. The kickoff alignments and calls are used almost every day in practice when players run conditioning sprints. This gives the coverage team (and the others) ample time to learn their correct alignments and assignments, while also getting into shape with the kickoff sprints.

Kamikaze Onside Kick Calls

The ''3'' call is shown in Diagram 8.2. The numbers of your coverage men will identify their responsibilities for the onside kick to the short, far-right zone. This zone, the favorite onside kick call, is the one that the kickoff team works on the most. The #1 coverage man becomes the *safety* after the ball is kicked and lays back behind the rush. The #2 and #3 men and the kicker converge on the ball as *contain*-men, making sure that the returner stays between the hash mark and the far sideline. Players #4, #5, #6, and #7 *go for the ball* at the shortest angle. The #8 and #9 men *block* the offensive men, numbered 4 and 5, respectively. They search them out, stay on them, and drive them away from the ball. Player #10 should be your fastest player, as he has probably the most important job of all—keeping the ball from going out of bounds and, if possible, recovering it. The kicker will try to kick the ball as hard as he can along the ground. He aims his toe at the top stripe on the ball, hoping to make it take two little hops and then a big one near the sideline and the opponent's forty-yard line.

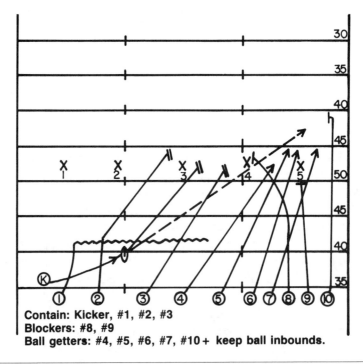

Diagram 8.2 Kamikaze ''3'' call onside kickoff.

The type of kick you choose to use will largely depend on what skills your kicker has. Accuracy is very important. You don't want the ball to end up on your side of the fifty-yard line, because your team has no chance of recovery and the other team gains excellent field position. You also do not want the kick to travel very deep into the opponent's territory, as they may be able to make a big return with the ball. Your kicker should work on hard, "squirmy," bouncy kicks with a lot of velocity. Diagram 8.2 illustrates the audible "3" call onside kick.

The second most prevalent call is a "1." A return team may cheat over to the 3 area if their scouting reports indicate that the ball is usually kicked to that area; this would leave the short left zone relatively vacant, and the kicker can then audible to that open area. With this call the #1 man becomes a main ball getter, responsible to keep the ball from going out of bounds. He should be the second fastest man on the squad. Players #2 and #3 block the offensive men numbered 1 and 2, driving them away from the ball. The kicker remains a contain-man along with #8 and #9, who were blockers in the "3" call. Player #10, the fastest man, becomes

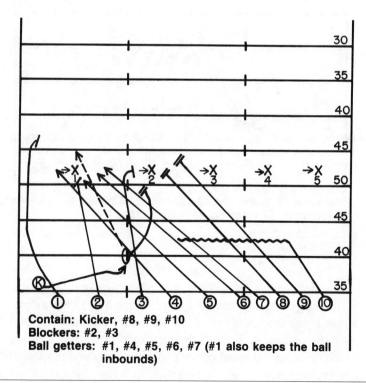

Contain: Kicker, #8, #9, #10
Blockers: #2, #3
Ball getters: #1, #4, #5, #6, #7 (#1 also keeps the ball inbounds)

Diagram 8.3 Kamikaze "1" call onside kickoff.

the safety. The #4, #5, #6, and #7 men again go for the ball at the fastest angle. The kicker will normally use a soccer-style kick to get the ball in the 1 area (see Diagram 8.3).

The ''2'' call is made least often on the onside kicks. Sometimes the scouting report shows that the middle man on the return team attacks aggressively to block the middle coverage man. With the opponent's middle man quickly taking himself out of the short area between the hash marks, an uncovered space or pocket is usually the result. The kicker attempts to place the ball directly behind the opponent's #3 man's position. The kicking team does not block the middle man, assuming he will take himself out of the play or that they will get to the ball before he does. Diagram 8.4 illustrates the ''2'' kickoff.

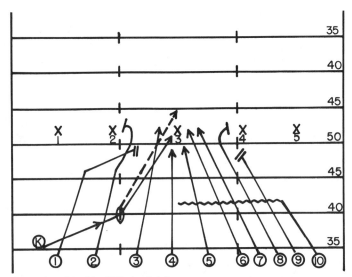

Contain: #1, #9, #10 (safety)
Blockers: #2 blocks the #2 opponent, #8 blocks #4 opponent.
Ball getters: The Kicker, #3, #4, #5, #6, #7

Diagram 8.4 Kamikaze ''2'' call onside kickoff.

The deep kickoffs are all covered with the same evenly spaced convergence. Three men are assigned between each hash mark and sideline, and four pursue down the middle. Every man except the safety (#10) follows contain-to-the-ball rules. Instruct them to keep good five-yard splits between each other and to avoid contact with blockers and immediately get back into their respective lanes. You want them to slide to the ball, staying square to the yard lines to ameliorate their lateral pursuit. The widest men, #1 and #9, never let the ball outside—they use the "five-by-five" rule, which instructs them to stay five yards outside *and* underneath the ball carrier. Diagram 8.5 shows the coverage tracks of the kickoff team when any deep kickoff (4, 5, or 6) has been called.

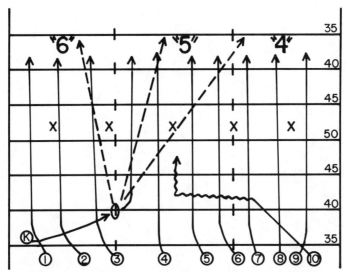

Everyone except the safety: sprint in lanes, contain to the ball carrier.

Diagram 8.5   Kamikaze deep kickoff.

Chapter 9

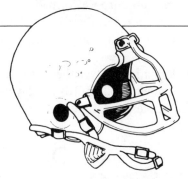

Utilizing the Defense's Multiplicity

So far we have emphasized the individual player components, such as alignments, responsibilities, and techniques, that are fundamental segments of a successful defense. Now we will look at the total schematic picture, addressing the defensive plan's usefulness and adaptability. The system's value should become more evident as you see the numerous adjustments being applied. This section illustrates just some of the defensive alignments, calls, and coverages that may be utilized from the multiple split package (except linebacker stunts and the goal line defense).

Standard Alignment Adjustments

Alignment variations, besides confusing the offensive blockers, allow your defenders to acquire a position advantage by shading the left or the right side or by aligning deeper or shallower, depending on defensive assignments. The multiple alignments, coverages, and blitz moves are grouped so as to better emphasize the use and diversification of the three defensive aspects.

44 "Omaha"

- A sound, balanced, all-purpose formation.
- Shown versus a Wing-T set, the defense's strength against the run (especially counters) and bootleg action passes make it a practical choice.
- The four defenders aligned over the inside three offensive men are in position to shut down another favorite play of this offense—the trap.
- Diagram 9.1 illustrates the alignment.

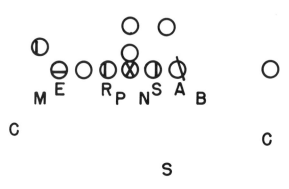

Diagram 9.1   44 Omaha alignment.

42 "Omaha"

- This call puts another defensive player to the side of formation strength.
- Pro "I" teams love to run the power pitch plays, and this alignment is up and ready in the right spots.
- The tailback cut-back (or sprint-draw) is another trademark of the "I"; Stud's (WDT) #2 alignment and Brutus's (WOLB) backside position provide a good defensive remedy.
- Diagram 9.2 illustrates the alignment.

24 "Omaha"

- A good adjustment to make when you need linebacker strength to one side and defensive lineman strength to the other.
- Diagram 9.3 illustrates the alignment: Assume that the wide side of the field is to the defense's left. The formation puts linemen into the short side and linebackers toward the wide side.

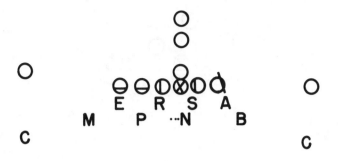

Diagram 9.2   42 Omaha alignment.

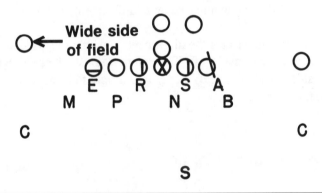

Diagram 9.3   24 Omaha alignment.

22 "Omaha"

- Strong alignment versus outside running and short passing teams.
- Inside linebackers can get outside fast and don't have to worry as much about inside draw play with their defensive tackles inside.
- Not a bad call on third-and-two when the offense is deciding versus a quick inside play or outside sweep.
- Diagram 9.4 illustrates the alignment.

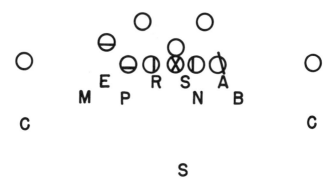

Diagram 9.4   22 Omaha alignment.

34 "Omaha" (+ "Squeeze")

- A good call when the offense aligns with the strength of the formation into the short side of the field.
- Maco (SOLB) is shown in a squeeze adjustment versus the tight-end-only side.
- Diagram 9.5 illustrates the alignment: Assume the wide side of the field is to the defense's left. The defense adjusts their strength to the wide side. Panther (IRLB) moves to the right to balance the offense's formation strength.

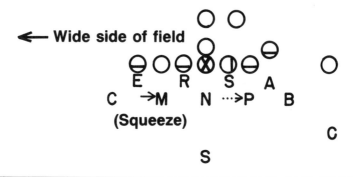

Diagram 9.5   34 Omaha alignment + squeeze.

33 "Omaha" (+ "Slide")

- Often called in passing situations to enable the defensive tackles to cover the gaps to both sides for the draw.

- With a spread offensive formation taking an inside linebacker to the outside, you are still in a sound alignment.
- Excellent long yardage call versus a strong-armed quarterback.
- Diagram 9.6 illustrates the alignment.

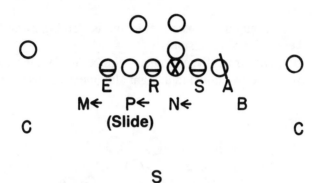

Diagram 9.6 33 Omaha alignment + slide.

11 (Stack) "Omaha"

- An aggressive penetrating (or slanting) alignment that you might choose in certain situations versus an option team or an opponent that relies on the base blocking dive attack.
- Good alignment if you feel quickness may be your best advantage.
- Good hash mark alignment when opponents put their strength and run to the wide side.
- Diagram 9.7 illustrates the alignment.

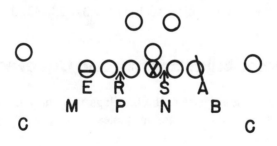

Diagram 9.7 11 Stack Omaha alignment.

11 (Slide) "Omaha"

- Similar to the "Stack" call but stronger versus offensive formations that show major alignment strength to one side or the other.
- Good call versus a veer team that places the strength of its formation to the wide side of the field.
- Good presnap alignment when your line is slanting away from the linebackers (to the weak side).
- Diagram 9.8 illustrates the alignment. Notice Ace (WDE) and Brutus (WOLB) must move down to a Tight alignment versus the tight end side.

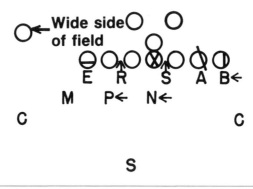

Diagram 9.8 11 Slide Omaha alignment.

There are quite a few other alignments that may be used for various reasons against the different offenses you will see during the season. We have used (sometimes quite often) the various defensive schemes devised with the numbered alignments, such as 13, 31, 23, 32, 34, and 41.

Special Adjustments and Coverages

To make understanding easier, the headings will show the adjustments in parentheses and the coverages in quotes.

(Tight) 42 "Omaha"

- The "Tight" call makes your base alignment stronger in the off-tackle area, and gives you a spot to align a relatively undisciplined ballplayer who happens to be very aggressive.

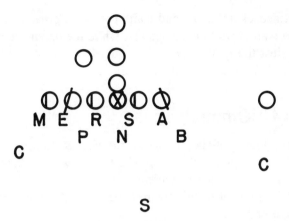

Diagram 9.9 **(Tight)** 42 "Omaha."

- This alignment allows your inside linebackers to roam virtually unhindered.
- Diagram 9.9 illustrates the alignment.

(Tight) 22 (Out) "Omaha"

- An excellent defensive formation versus opponents with superior speed.
- Your corners are strengthened with the aggressive position of your outside linebackers close to the line of scrimmage. With the "Omaha" call (and possible "Raider" call to the tight end side), the outside linebackers will attack action to their side very quickly.

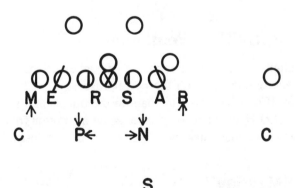

Diagram 9.10 **(Tight)** 22 (Out) "Omaha."

- Inside linebackers' depth and width provide a great starting point to run down all plays to their outside, while the defensive tackles protect against the quick trap.
- Diagram 9.10 illustrates the alignment.

(Wide) 44 "Omaha"

- The "original split-six" is one of the best containment alignments in the defensive playbook. It is similar to the "wide-tackle-six," which also is a flank-defending scheme.
- A super alignment to blitz from because of the containment of the defensive ends.
- If an option team is too good to beat with the read-and-react approach, get after them with the "Wide" look.
- Diagram 9.11 illustrates the alignment.

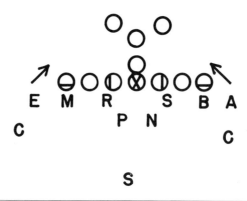

Diagram 9.11   (Wide) 44 "Omaha."

(Wide) 42 (Sniff) "Weak Mayday"

- Good alignment versus an opponent with an excellent split-end passing attack, combined with the power rushes.
- Panther (IRLB) has room to roam in the opponent's strength area.
- Panther (IRLB) could be assigned to cover all motion from this setup.
- Diagram 9.12 illustrates the alignment with a "Rosey" call.

44 (In) "Mayday"

- A very safe outside alignment with blitz potential to the inside.

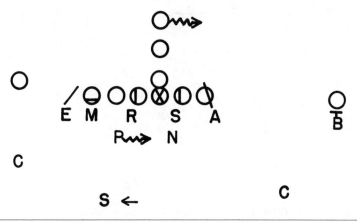

Diagram 9.12   (Wide) 42 (Sniff) "Weak Mayday," "Rosey" call.

- You can aggressively attack the inside running game and the drop-back quarterback while bending with outside screens or picking off the short slant pass.
- Not a bad defense versus the run-and-shoot team with a great runner at fullback.
- Diagram 9.13 illustrates the alignment.

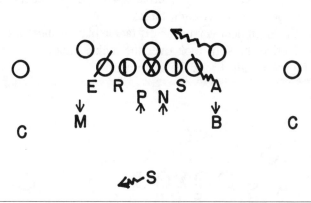

Diagram 9.13   44 (In) "Mayday."

33 (Zigzag) "Strong Mayday"

- Good call versus the "double-twins" offense.
- Zigzag provides tough linebacker run support to one side and good curl-flat coverage to the other side.

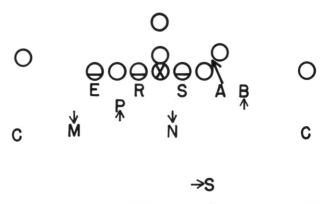

Diagram 9.14 33 (**Zigzag**) ''Strong Mayday,'' ''Lucy'' call.

- The safety can cheat out to the outside where the two receivers provide the immediate threat.
- Diagram 9.14 illustrates the alignment.

24 (Up) ''Omaha-Raider''

- This is an aggressive run-stopper formation.
- To the tight end side the cornerback will quickly react to action his way and join the front-eight attack.
- Dynamite alignment versus the off-tackle play in short yardage situations. Notice the split look over the tackle area.
- Diagram 9.15 illustrates the alignment.

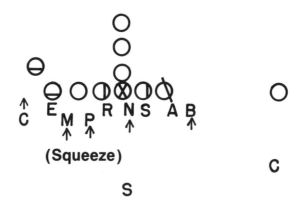

Diagram 9.15 24 (Up) ''Omaha-Raider.''

43 (Slide-Back) "Mayday"

- The slide could be an automatic adjustment to the Trips, while the "Back" call puts the linebackers in a good pass-prevent position.
- The 43 alignment balances the offense's running strength, while the linebackers balance the pass threat.
- Excellent third-and-five call with the ball on the hash mark.
- Diagram 9.16 illustrates the alignment.

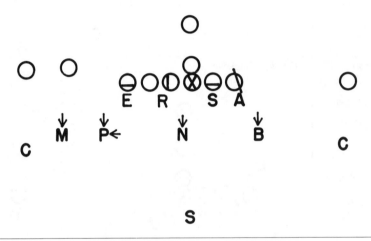

Diagram 9.16   43 (Slide-Back) "Mayday."

41 (Back) "Buckeye"

- With the Back adjustment all five underneath defenders drop back off the line of scrimmage five or six yards.
- Good call versus opponents with skilled wide receivers.
- Another third-and-long defense that covers by alignment the big-threat plays—screens, draws, reverses, etc.
- Diagram 9.17 illustrates the alignment.

(Tight) 22 (Up) "Buckeye"

- This alignment allows you to attack and jam the wide-outs at the same time.
- Not a bad "surprise" alignment in a first-and-ten situation.

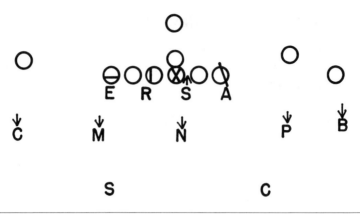

Diagram 9.17 41 (Back) "Buckeye."

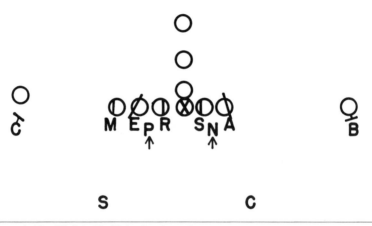

Diagram 9.18 (Tight) 22 (Up) "Buckeye."

- This might even be used in short yardage situations, especially versus the proficient short-passing combination of quarterback and wide receivers.
- Diagram 9.18 illustrates the alignment.

Adding the "Four-Down" Movements to the Call

Defensive adjustments utilizing the movement of the defensive linemen add another diversification to the calls.

33 (Slant Strong) "Omaha"

- A good hash mark call to get defensive linemen moving to the wide side of the field on the snap of the ball.
- Slants prove beneficial with good scouting reports and opponents with strong tendencies.
- Slants may enable a lesser athlete to equalize the situation.
- Diagram 9.19 illustrates the defensive attack.

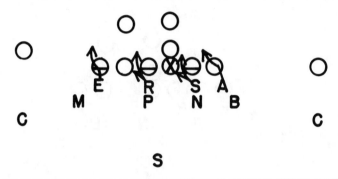

Diagram 9.19   33 (Slant Strong) "Omaha," "Looks good" call.

24 (Flip) "Buckeye"

- Provides for an excellent pass rush advantage.
- Great change-up to the normal read-and-react approach.
- Allows half of your front-four to take a chance, while the others are reading offensive movement.
- Diagram 9.20 illustrates the move.

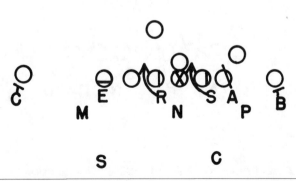

Diagram 9.20   24 (Flip) "Buckeye."

42 (Rat-Shoot) ''Omaha''

- This move typically catches the offensive blockers by surprise because the defensive tackle usually delivers a blow from his ''shade'' advantage.
- You may allow your defensive tackles to perform this move on their own when they sense that they can get past their blocker.
- The inside linebackers check inside trap before doing anything else.
- Diagram 9.21 illustrates the defensive tackle's action.

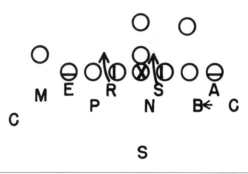

Diagram 9.21   42 (Rat-Shoot) ''Mayday.''

22 (Crash) ''Omaha''

- This move really puts the tight ends in a predicament; if they attempt to block the defensive end's outside, they may lose him to the inside, but if they block straight ahead, they can't control the flanks.

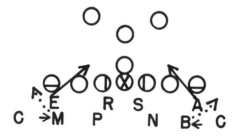

Diagram 9.22   22 (Crash) ''Omaha'' and possible ''Squeeze Raider'' call.

- This is an excellent call when you expect an outside option attack, whether the sprint option, the outside veer, or the basic dive option.
- Good short yardage call when you have to "make something happen."
- Diagram 9.22 demonstrates the move. Versus this formation the defense would probably squeeze down and call a Raider coverage to both sides.

Chapter 10

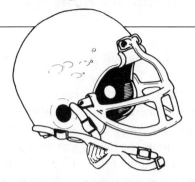

Defensive Contortions and Distortions

Most coaches, I am sure, would agree that any football team tends to become a reflection of its coach's personality. It would seem logical for that personality also to be reflected in the type of defense the coach chooses to run. By and large, "conventional" coaches choose standard, orthodox defenses; "conservative" coaches use conservative tactics; "aggressive" coaches take more chances; and some coaches just look at defense as something to put up with between offensive possessions of the ball. Certain coaches might like to consider themselves somewhat nonconformist, or maybe a breed apart from other coaches. They might feel that they have a little more "artistic" blood in their veins, and they enjoy the schematic aspects of the defensive game. They secretly may envision themselves as football's defensive version of Bill Walsh, the San Francisco 49ers offensive genius.

Such adventurist-type coaches may be particularly interested in this section of the book. The *contortions* and *distortions* are not off-the-wall, fabricated defensive alignments. They are unique, to a degree, but they are sound in principle and they have been used successfully. This chapter will attempt to expand your defensive repertoire by supplying sound and usable, yet unorthodox, formations. These varieties of defensive attacks come illustrated as well as defined.

Using Defensive Alignment Distortions to Your Advantage

The first defensive alignment distortions shown were developed to get the split look over the offensive guard area, as well as the standard split over the offensive center area. The defensive system already can acquire the split look over the offensive tackle's area by squeezing-down the outside linebacker in certain numbered defensive alignments; the Split alignment positioned over the offensive guards adds the ability to use the split's advantages anywhere along the line of scrimmage. Two defensive adjustments have been devised; one of them (*Rip*) puts the split over the offensive weak guard. The other alignment (*Stud*) puts the split over the offensive strong guard. The alignments were given the same names as the two defensive tackles because the call tells those two defenders on which side of the ball to align. The defenses are explained later in separate sections.

Defensive Distortions Dealing with Alignment

Your defensive personnel need to understand that although these alignments are unusual, they are not just some crazy attempt to be different. These alignments are similar to adjustments made by many other teams, including big-time colleges and pros. This fact should add credibility to help your players to believe in what you as a coach have installed. The first distortion to be discussed moves the split in the defensive alignment over one of the offensive guards, rather than the offensive center. The Rip defensive formation is shown in Diagram 10.1, with defensive personnel reacting to basic plays. Moving the defensive line to the strength of the formation while the split aligns over the offense's weakside guard is a good distortion to start with. (Again, headings list the adjustments in parentheses and the coverages in quotes.)

(Rip) ''Omaha''

The call of ''Rip'' tells your strongside defensive tackle, Rip, to align in a #3 position on the offensive tackle to the strong side. Conversely, Stud, the weakside defensive tackle, aligns in a #3 position on the weak-

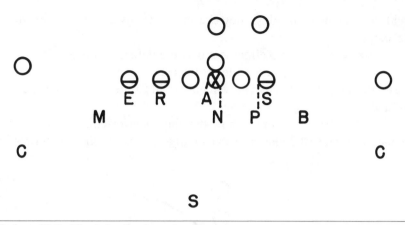

Diagram 10.1   The defensive formation Rip.

side offensive tackle. The call informs Ace, the weakside defensive end, to move inside to the strongside A gap. He will align on the center's strongside shoulder, threatening the gap. Ace (WDE) is usually the perfect type of athlete to man the "semi-noseguard" position, since his aggressiveness and quickness led to his being picked as a defensive end. The inside linebackers now slide to the weak side covering the A and B gaps; combined

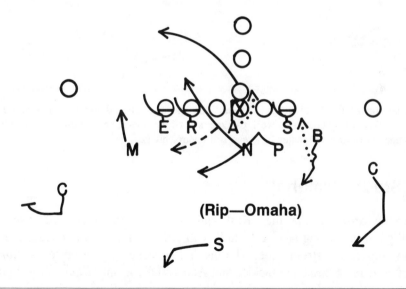

(Rip—Omaha)

Diagram 10.2a   In this (Rip) "Omaha," the offensive action is going to the strong side. Nasty (ILB) has a scrape-hole in the onside B gap, and Evil (SE) aligns in a #3 position on the tight end.

with the defensive tackles, they create a defensive alignment mismatch in the area.

As can be seen, a Rip alignment puts the defensive lineman's strength to the offense's strong side while the linebackers favor the weak side. The basic reactions to offensive movement are illustrated in Diagrams 10.2a, b, and c.

Diagrams 10.2a, b, and c show the alignment reacting to direction of a play. Diagram 10.3 illustrates the use of a blitz call from a Rip formation.

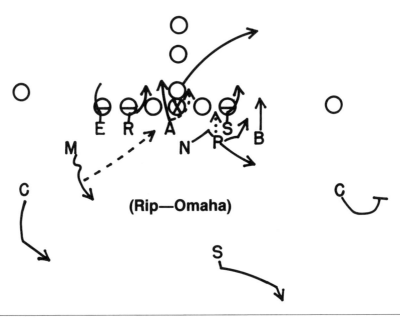

(Rip—Omaha)

Diagram 10.2b In this (Rip) "Omaha," the offensive action is going to the weak side. Ace (WDE) may be able to work past the nose of the center; he is allowed to angle his stance in toward the center if he can still control his gap.

(Stud) "Omaha"

In the same way that the "Rip" call told your defensive tackle, Rip, to align to the strong side, a "Stud" call tells your weakside tackle, Stud, to align to the strong side. The inside linebackers again go to the *same side as their* weakside tackle, and Ace (WDE) again *aligns to the same side* as the strongside defensive tackle (*Rip*), *who aligns to the weak side*. You now have an alignment with the "split" positioned over the strong-side offensive guard. This is the only call that puts Rip (SDT) to the weak side and Stud (WDT) to the strong side. This defensive alignment will

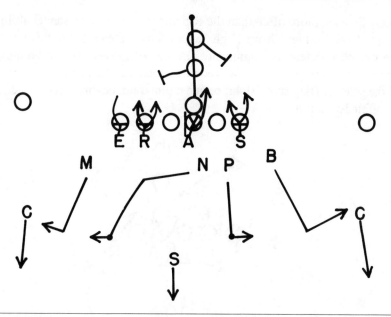

Diagram 10.2c In this (Rip) "Omaha," Ace (WDE) and Stud (WDT) exchange pass rush responsibilities. Ace can rush either A gap on the drop-back pass.

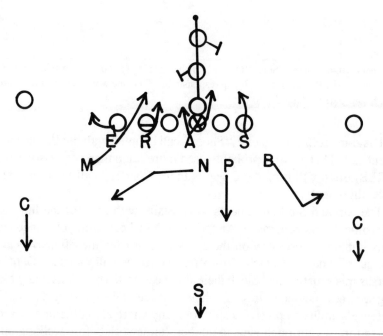

Diagram 10.3 A "Rip Charlie Omaha" call with a one-linebacker blitz move that is used quite often with the (Rip) "Omaha" call.

likely be used more often than the Rip alignment. The personnel abilities of our 1979 Cottage Grove High School football team led to this becoming our base defensive alignment. The 1979 Lions proved to be quite a successful team, posting a 10-2 record, the best in the eighty-year history of the school. Diagrams 10.4a, b, and c illustrate the three basic reactions to offensive actions.

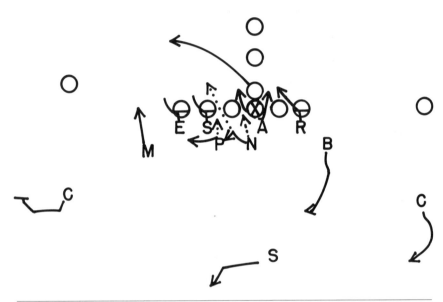

Diagram 10.4a   In this (Stud) "Omaha" the ball goes toward the strong side. Nasty (ILB) or Panther (IRLB) can be given B gap responsibility. The one who does not attack through the B gap pursues laterally to the ball.

Diagram 10.5 illustrates a "Shoot" call coupled with the "Stud" alignment call. This move is probably used more often than not. Also, Panther (IRLB) often will blitz the C gap with a "Charlie" call from this defensive alignment.

The Rip and Stud alignments work easily with most of the linebacker adjustments and coverages. An "Up" or "In" call with your linebackers puts immediate pressure on the blocking rules for the offensive center, the guard, and the tackle. Most offensive teams will make a "Gap" call versus this situation and block their assigned gaps. This limits many blocking schemes and opens up scrape-holes outside of the threatened area. Your defense's ability to present a split look anywhere along the line of scrimmage forces your opponents to do their homework before walking out on the field.

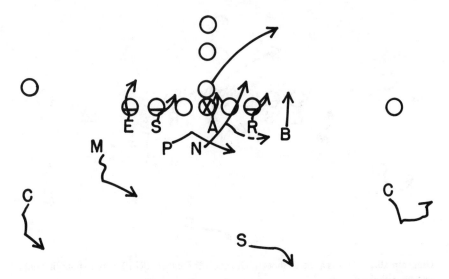

Diagram 10.4b A (Stud) "Omaha" with Nasty (ILB) again having the B gap for a scrape lane when the ball goes to the offense's weak side. Panther (IRLB) checks the backside A gap.

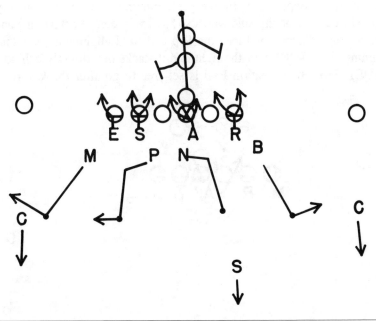

Diagram 10.4c A (Stud) "Omaha" with the drop-back pass and Ace (WDE) and Rip (SDT) exchanging assignments.

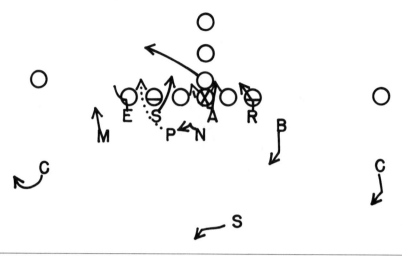

Diagram 10.5 This is a (Stud-Shoot) "Omaha." If Panther (IRLB) were to blitz, it would just be called "Charlie."

Now we go one step farther with the Rip and Stud alignments and plans. The *Viking* scheme developed from a need to have a defense that could blitz while still allowing a seven-spoke coverage design. This set may help you versus an opponent with one great running back, who (logically) is given the ball repeatedly, and who also has a very competent passing attack. The Viking scheme combines the Rip and Stud alignments, but instead of lining Evil (SDE) over the tight end it stacks him directly behind Ace (WDE). From this position Evil is set free to go after the key running

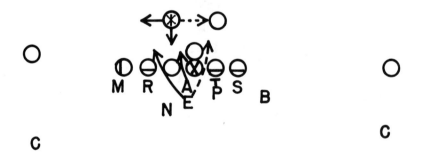

Diagram 10.6a (Rip-Viking) "Omaha."

back. Scrape-holes are created for him. This scheme is combined with Omaha and Buckeye coverages. Diagram 10.6a and b illustrate the combinations used most often, along with some coaching hints that help make the coverage work.

(Rip-Viking) "Omaha"

Notice that Panther (IRLB) must align close to the offensive weak guard to "bait" the guard into blocking him, which creates a lane for Evil. Evil (SDE) is shown in Diagram 10.6a keying the near halfback and will attack whichever side the back goes to.

(Stud-Viking) "Buckeye"

Stud-Viking goes good with "Buckeye" coverage because Nasty (ILB) is positioned to the deeper weak side where he can help in the void created by Brutus' (WOLB) wide alignment. Panther (IRLB) aligns tight to the strongside guard to draw his block (Diagram 10.6b).

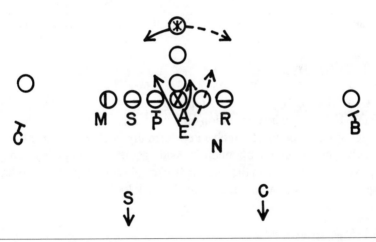

Diagram 10.6b   (Stud-Viking) "Buckeye."

40 "Omaha"

The 40 alignment is not really unusual. It is called most often when you want to cover both the center and the guard. This is a good adjustment to make versus good trapping teams or those that rely on pulling guards to lead their outside attack. When Stud (WDT) aligns in his 0 position on the nose of the center, Ace (WDE) has to cheat down to a #3 alignment on the weakside offensive tackle. You may choose to have Ace play the nose position and Stud remain outside on the offensive tackle. This develops an excellent scrape-hole between the two defensive tackles. Stud favors the weakside gap. Diagram 10.7 illustrates the "40" call with Nasty attacking through the onside A gap.

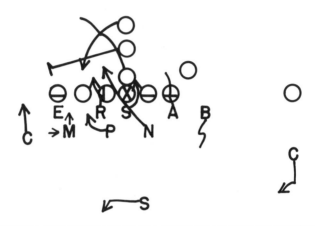

Diagram 10.7   In this 40 "Omaha," Maco (SOLB) is in a squeeze adjustment.

404 "Omaha"

To get a "double-40" look it is simpler to call "404." The "zero" directs Ace (WDE) to align in a 0 position on the offensive center. With this defensive set at least one inside linebacker normally is blitzed. This alignment virtually shuts down the opponent's inside game and can give you a great drop-back pass rush with the one linebacker blitzing. Diagrams 10.8a and b illustrate two standard calls from the 404 look.

404 "Buckeye"

The 404 alignment is a great combination with two-deep Buckeye coverage. You can jam and cover all the receivers and still get a great rush on the passer. This could be an excellent change-up to your prevent defense when the offense is moving the ball. Diagram 10.8b illustrates this defensive set versus a shotgun offense setup. An "Able" call by Nasty (ILB) informs the defensive linemen that he will blitz his A gap.

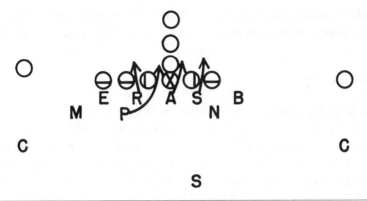

Diagram 10.8a In this 404 "Omaha," Panther (IRLB) blitzes with an "Ace" call, and both defensive tackles, as well as Ace (WDE), react appropriately to the call.

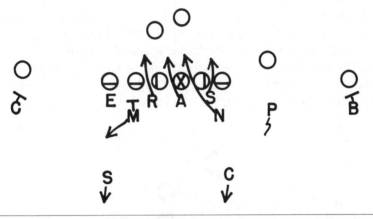

Diagram 10.8b A hard inside rush is coupled with good containment on the perimeter.

Defensive Distortions Dealing With Movement

Movement by the defensive personnel just before the snap of the ball can be very confusing to the offensive blockers. Conversely, movement can also prove harmful to the defense when the defender finds himself in a position where he cannot fend off the offensive blocker and pursue the ball. For this reason, movement distortions should be well polished and utilized only in certain situations, for example, when the offense is methodically moving the ball down the field and you want to break their rhythm.

Another situation might be the result of a coach's decision to utilize his small, quick players more productively against a bigger, slower opponent.

"Up-Jump"

This move has proved effective with the linebacker's "Up" call, which puts all four linebackers up about a yard from the line of scrimmage. This is a threatening alignment and usually results in last-second calls by the offensive line to be able to block the possible linebacker blitzes. Adding the *Jump* move to the alignment simply allows the linebackers to move quickly back to a position where they can pursue to the ball without getting walled off. The linebackers alter their normal stance so that their outside foot is well behind them, to facilitate moving backward on the snap of the ball.

The Jump moves correspond to the defensive coverage being used. If you are in an Omaha alignment where you would rotate up to the action of the ball, the outside-onside linebacker attacks the play from his Up position. The remaining linebackers quickly shuffle back a few yards and then proceed to their normal pursuit angles. In a Mayday coverage, where the outside linebackers go to their flat area on action on their side, the onside-

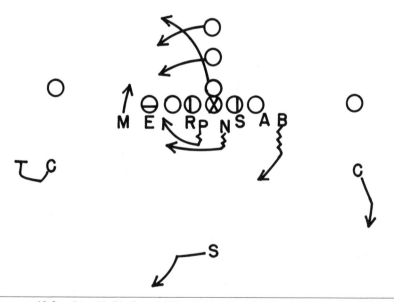

Diagram 10.9a In a 44 (Up-Jump) "Omaha" call against key action to the defense's left, the inside linebackers get right back into their normal pursuit angles after quickly shuffling back from their up position.

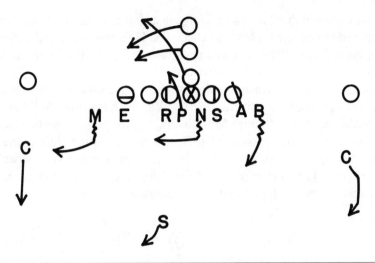

Diagram 10.9b In a 44 (Up-Jump) "Mayday" call against key action to the defense's left, Panther (IRLB), the onside inside linebacker, attacks while the onside outside linebacker retreats to the flat area.

inside linebacker would attack from his Up position and the others would quickly retreat a couple of steps. Diagrams 10.9a and b illustrate the Up-Jump move used with Omaha and Mayday coverages.

Other calls may be made with the Up-Jump move. Any linebacker's name may be called with this alignment, which instructs that player to blitz no matter what action the offense shows. Also, your linebackers may

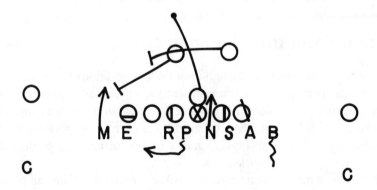

Diagram 10.10 A 44 (Up-Jump-Nasty) "Omaha" call.

choose to crowd the line of scrimmage in a similar manner when a Kansas (Man-to-Man coverage) blitz is called. The Up-Jump move will definitely keep the offense off-balance and tentative. Diagram 10.10 illustrates the Up-Jump with Nasty (ILB) being called to blitz.

An example of the Up-Jump alignment or move used with the multiple blitz moves is shown in Diagram 10.11. With a "Kansas-MoBy" (outside-linebacker blitz with Man-to-Man coverage) call, your inside linebackers may use tactics similar to their Up-Jump move and align close to the line of scrimmage, only to back out at the same time the outside linebackers are blitzing. The linebackers start from the In alignment, but the inside linebacker's move is similar to the Up-Jump reaction.

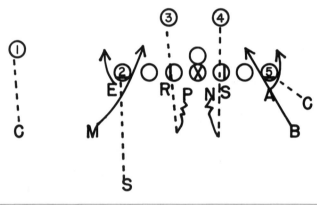

Diagram 10.11   In a 44 (In) "Kansas-Moby" call, the inside linebackers' alignment and movement resemble the Up-Jump. Both outside linebackers call "Charlie."

Slants From the 11 Alignment

One of the most effective, though unorthodox, additions to our defensive package has been defensive lineman slants from the gap alignments. Normally, the desired position for a defensive lineman prior to a slant move is head-up with his opponent, because he is in the best position to slant to either his inside or his outside gap, with less distance to go than if he were lined up on the blocker's shoulder.

However, it has been our experience that slanting from the gap position can be even more effective than the head-up position. As every coach knows, a gap alignment is used to get defensive penetration. Consequently, the offensive linemen are taught to deny the penetration by blocking down at a sharp angle to get in front of the defender's charge. With the offensive man blocking hard to his inside gap, it is easy for the defensive lineman to slant around his block. This action is similar to slanting to the inside, because the offensive blocker to the outside is unable to block the defensive lineman, and the inside blocker also must block back at a severe angle. Diagrams 10.12a, b, and c demonstrate three slant moves with the offensive blockers put at a disadvantage because of the gap alignment.

Diagram 10.12a   The defender slants to the outside around the lineman's gap block.

Diagram 10.12b   The inside lineman blocks back at a sharp angle, and the defender loops inside.

Diagram 10.12c   The outside lineman tries to secure the backside, but he is unable to get to the slanting lineman.

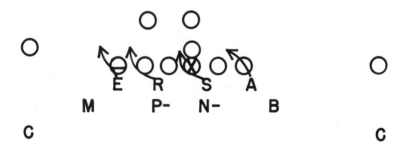

Diagram 10.13a   In an 11 (Slant-Strong) "Omaha," Nasty (ILB) yells "Looks good" after seeing the strength of the formation.

Diagrams 10.13a and b show two examples of the 11 Slant defense. Remember that the linebacker's call of "Looks good" means to slant left and "Ready, ready" means to slant right. Most slant calls are signaled just as strong or weak, with the linebackers making the judgment of which direction after the opponents line up in their formation.

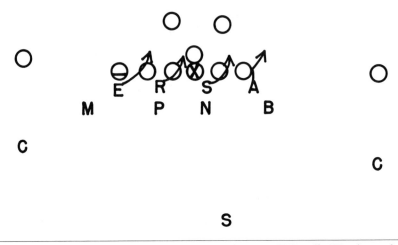

Diagram 10.13b In an 11 (Slant-Weak) "Omaha," Nasty (ILB) yells "Ready, ready" after seeing the strength of the formation.

Chapter 11

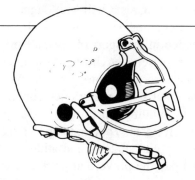

"Domino" Drills

Recently, I was witness to an impressive spectacle. Thousands of dominoes were set on edge in countless rows. Each domino had been painted a particular color on the side that would be exposed when it was tipped over. Hundreds of Japanese students had diligently worked, nearly around the clock, for over a month to set up the show. When the big moment arrived, one domino was tipped over, and a magnificent chain reaction ensued. The action of the dominoes knocking one another over lasted only about five minutes, but it culminated in a beautiful 10,000-square-foot collage. This extraordinary display was matched in value only by its remarkable development.

Being a typical football coach, with Xs and Os continually running through my head, I was drawn by the seemingly significant correlation between this event and the game of football. Like the domino art, the value of football is not found just in the short span of the actual competition or in the final score. Coincidentally, the actual playing time of a typical football game approximates the time it took the dominoes to finish their chain reaction. For a dedicated athlete, just five minutes a week of "value" would be hard to justify, and given an entire year, he would only accumulate about an hour's worth of "worthwhile experiences."

As far as the final outcome, or winning, being the only objective, it is obvious that for every game where there is a winner, there must also be a loser. A grade of 50 percent will get you an "F" in most any class-room subject. Without getting carried away with analogies, I want to suggest that the real value in the sport of football involves the intrinsic as well as the extrinsic experiences. The dedication, the sacrifice, the effort, the practice, the successes, the failures, and so on, are the true benefits. How you get to the final score really does count. This is the approach that we have taken to building our program. Our players are taught that the game is a total involvement. They do things "right": They obey training rules; they are good, polite students and athletes; they hustle and work hard in practice and pay the proverbial price it takes to be winners. We refer to this as "earning the win." We hope with this approach that the values gained from playing the sport of football will remain with our athletes for the rest of their lives.

Like the dominoes, the essentials, or fundamentals, of football are inter-dependent. Before you can successfully execute a defensive scheme, you need players with the proper attitude, physical condition, and fundamental skills. The Super Split defense is not magic—it works on the same premise as every other defensive approach. To bring this philosophy into your prac-tice design, you have to organize your practice schedules so that you teach or improve the most fundamental skills before adding the frills. Decisions concerning selection of drills and time involvement should keep drill variety to a minimum to give your players increased practice time to improve the most necessary, basic skills. The front-eight defensive players in a multiple alignment defense will not have sufficient time to practice each alignment's technique variation with equal emphasis. Therefore, the skills to be used most often should be practiced most. The same can be said for your line-backers in the multiple alignment defenses. For example, your defensive tackles should work hard on the #4 alignment technique, while the defen-sive ends emphasize #3. The inside linebackers would perform most of their practice repetitions from the inside (44) alignment.

Systematic Practice Schedules

Practice schedules during a game week are designated according to the main objective of each day's practice. The practice schedule usually run on Monday is referred to as *Big O,* because offensive improvement is the primary objective. Tuesday is dubbed *Big D*, because defense is the forte of the day. Wednesday's plan is called *Polish,* as we put the final offensive and defensive plans into practice. Thursday's practice schedule is *Hay-Day,* referring to the fact that the practice "hay" is "in the barn." We go over final adjustments, the complete kicking game, etc.

These schedules are what you might call the master plan of the domino procedure. For defense the first major practice day is Tuesday, but the first fundamentals of defensive play are practiced on Monday. These fundamentals include stance and proper movement to the ball. The defensive portion of Monday's practice also includes basic alignments and adjustments that the defense will use versus the upcoming opponents. At the end of a typical Big O practice, the defense will perform the Team Pursuit conditioning drill.

The following defensive drills are run on whatever day they are normally scheduled. Of course, they do not have to be limited to just one particular day or practice schedule; they should be inserted as the time and place make them most practical.

Monday's Practice Drills: ("Big O")

Includes

- Stance drills
- Movement drills (front-eight and seven-spokes)
- Alignment adjustments for Friday's opponent
- Team Pursuit conditioning drill

Systematic Stance Drill: Defensive Linemen, Three-Point Stance

Step 1.   Align double-arm's distance apart, facing the coach, with toes on the yard line.

Step 2.   The inside of the feet are just outside the width of the shoulders; toes are pointed straight ahead.

Step 3.   Bending at the waist, players put their elbows on their knees, making sure that back and shoulders are parallel to the ground. Diagram 11.1a illustrates the proper stance.

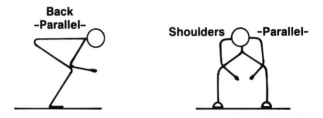

Diagram 11.1a   Front and side views of the initial position before the three-point stance.

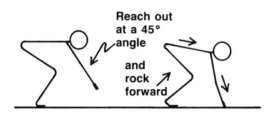

Diagram 11.1b   Rocking forward from the two-point to the three-point stance.

Step 4.   From this position they reach out at approximately a 45° angle (with the right arm, assuming a right-handed stance), and slowly rock forward until their fingers are on the ground. Diagram 11.1b illustrates this action.

Step 5.   When their fingers are on the ground, they lift their heads and straighten their backs.

Some good coaching points may help players who have difficulty getting into a good three-point stance:

- The right hand should be just under and to the right of their eyes.
- Their heels should have air under them. (A toe-to-heel stagger of the right foot is a common adjustment for defensive linemen—some take even a little bigger stagger.)
- The head should be up, with the neck "in cement." The players should be looking "through their eyebrows," and if they can't see at least three yards ahead, the buttocks are too high. If they can see more than seven or so yards ahead, the hips are probably too low.
- Proper weight on the support arm can be tested by quickly pulling the hand off the ground. If the player falls, boom!, he probably had too much weight on his hand. If he doesn't fall at all, he didn't have enough weight there.

- Check the angle of the bend in the legs. The proper angle is close to 90°—with any less, it becomes difficult to come quickly out of the stance. With any more angle, they cannot get enough explosive "uncoiling" action. Diagram 11.1c illustrates the side view of a defensive lineman's basic three-point stance.

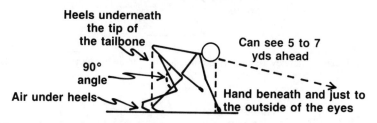

Diagram 11.1c Side view of the three-point stance—the right hand is down, and the left arm is resting on the left knee.

Systematic Stance Drill: Linebackers, Two-Point Stance

Step 1. Align double-arm's distance apart, facing the coach, with toes on the yard line.

Step 2. The insides of the feet are just outside the width of the shoulders; toes are pointed straight ahead.

Step 3. Bending at the waist, players put their hands on their knees, keeping shoulders over the knees and arms straight. (At this point it is important to check the player's lower back. Is it straight? There should be an arch there. This is called "unlocking the hips," and some players have a hard time acquiring this form. It usually helps to tell them to push their buttocks back. A straight back enables delivery of a good, hard defensive blow or tackle.) Diagram 11.2a illustrates Step 3.

Step 4. The next systematic move is to have players slide their hands off the front of their knees, which will drop the shoulders and hips lower. In this stance their backs are now at about a 20° angle to the ground. The angle in the bend of the legs is reduced to a little over 90°.

Step 5. Players float their heels so that the weight is on the balls of their feet and they bring their elbows inside of their knees. (If you were to drop a string from the tip of a player's "tail," it should land a few inches behind his heels.) Diagram 11.2b illustrates the linebacker's two-point stance.

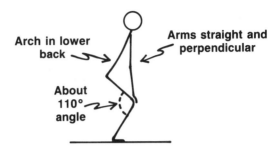

Diagram 11.2a Side view of a figure before moving into an aggressive two-point stance.

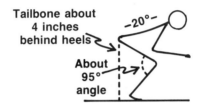

Diagram 11.2b Side view of a figure in an aggressive two-point stance.

Systematic Stance Drill: Secondary, Two-Point Stance

The secondary's Systematic Stance Drill is set up differently from the others; players start the drill facing the sideline and the coach while straddling the yard line. You will normally use about four different yard lines (e.g., the ten-, fifteen-, twenty-, and twenty-five-yard lines), and the players stack approximately three yards behind each other. The drill is started with the players' feet pointed at a 45° angle to their right as they face the sideline. Diagram 11.3a illustrates the position of the defensive back's head, shoulders, and feet when initiating the drill. Diagram 11.3b illustrates the drill setup with the entire group.

Step 1. Place the right heel and the left toe on the line being straddled.

Step 2. The insides of the feet are just outside the width of the shoulders. Toes are pointed straight at a 45° angle from the sideline to the player's right.

Step 3. Bending at the waist, players put their hands on their knees, keeping their shoulders over the knees and their arms straight. Check to

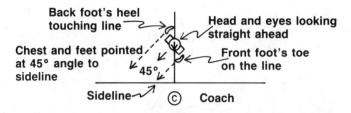

Diagram 11.3a   Top view of a defensive back in proper position to start the secondary's Systematic Stance Drill.

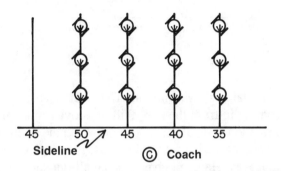

Diagram 11.3b   The twelve defensive backs are lined up on their respective yard lines, approximately three yards behind one another, awaiting the start of the Systematic Stance Drill. The dashes on each side of the circles represent the backs' feet.

see that the player's chest and shoulders are also pointing at a 45° angle to his right. The head and eyes are pointed straight down the yard line at the coach. Also check the defensive backs to be sure their backs are arched.

Step 4.   As the secondary player slides his hands off the front of his knees, he does not assume as low a stance as did the linebackers. The slope from his shoulders to his hips is about 70°, and the bend in his legs is just slight, about 130° (with 180° being straight). Coaches should check that the stances are very relaxed and that most of the weight is distributed over the back leg. Diagram 11.3c illustrates the defensive back's basic two-point stance.

Movement Drills: (Front-Eight)

It has been shown that athletes are able to learn or improve physical skills much quicker if the movements are performed under conditions requiring

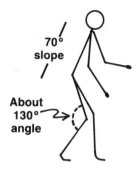

70°
slope

About
130°
angle

Diagram 11.3c Side view of a figure in a relaxed two-point stance, ready to retreat at the snap of the ball.

less speed and utilizing slower motion. The brain is able to compute the information coming in from the new skill or activity much more readily when that information is regulated at a speed which the brain can manage. After the skills are learned at reduced speeds, they can be accelerated as proficiency improves. Having players use an all-out sprint in all of their drills may get them in shape, but they do not acquire the desired skill levels as quickly.

As discussed concerning the ART of defense, the form with which players perform their various skills is very important. Good form is a forerunner of good technique. Consequently, movement and skill drills should be performed under controlled speeds, using perfect form. The speed of the drills will pick up naturally as players begin to master the skills.

"Struts" Drill: Defensive Linemen

As simple as it may seem, the defensive linemen need to practice coming out of their stance. This drill is also used with offensive linemen and backs. We have named this action *struts,* and it is coupled with the Systematic Stance Drill.

Step 1.   Starting from a (right-handed) three-point stance, the player on the coach's command of "one" takes a short (the length of one foot) step with his right foot. His right arm moves backward and his left arm forward in basic running-movement form. When taking this first step the player should *not* raise his shoulder or head, narrow his base (his stance width), or take a long step.

Step 2.   On the coach's command of "two," the player takes a short step with his left foot, moving his left arm backward and his right arm forward. His shoulders and head rise just slightly, and he maintains his base width as his strides become longer.

Step 3.   On the commands of "three" and "four," the players take alternating steps, while maintaining the wide base and low form.

Step 4.   After taking the fourth step, the players jog on out, gradually raising their shoulders and narrowing their running base until they are running naturally with good form.

The essence of this drill is in these points, which should be accentuated: Players do not stand up, take long strides, or narrow their base when coming out of their stances. This drill has vastly improved our players' ability to come off the ball and to make successful contact with their opponents. The drill is normally done in lines of four; when done repeatedly in preseason practices, it shows great results.

"Starts" Drill: Defensive Linemen (Lateral Movement)

Although lateral movement skills are important for all defensive football players, they are crucial for the front-eight defenders. Skillful lateral movement is paramount for defensive linemen and linebackers, meaning they must practice these movements much more often than the defensive secondary. The Starts Drill is especially beneficial to the defensive linemen because of their short distance from their opponent and their need to stay very low while moving laterally along the line of scrimmage.

To set up for the Starts Drill, place four heavy bags on yard stripes five yards apart (lay the bags on their sides, lengthwise with the yard stripes). Place a cone on the five-yard stripe outside of each end bag. The coach positions himself with a ball behind and in the middle of the four bags. Like other drills that utilize the yard lines for setup, this is a good one to perform at the junction of yard lines with the sideline.

Step 1.   The first line of players (usually the defensive ends on the outside and the defensive tackles on the inside) line up one foot from the end of the bags. The position they take on the bag can be a #4, #3, or #2 alignment, whichever they feel they need to work from.

Step 2.   Upon movement of the ball from the ground by the coach, the defensive players strike a defensive blow on the end of the bags. (If they are using the tripod method, they use a two-hand shiver on the end of the bag; if they are using a flipper technique, they drop their flipper-side knee to the ground as they deliver the blow.)

Step 3.   As soon as the coach lifts the ball off the ground, he points it either to the left or to the right. The four linemen shuffle (using perfect form—staying low, feet wide, elbows inside, shoulders square to the line of scrimmage) laterally along the bags, giving each a shiver as they pass.

Step 4. When they have shuffled past the last bag (to the cone), they drop their outside knee and do a hip roll.

The defensive lineman on the outside bag toward the direction of the lateral movement comes to the cone right away, while the defender to the far side has to shiver all four bags before coming to the cone. You can even this up by having the defenders serpentine back to the bags so that they end up on the side opposite from where they started. Each group does at least two repetitions to the right and two to the left. The coach may also indicate "pass" after lifting the ball from the ground by quickly raising the ball over his head. The defenders respond to his move by delivering a blow, then rushing directly over the bag (straddling it) to the coach, who points to a cone to instruct them to move laterally in that direction. Diagram 11.4 illustrates the drill design.

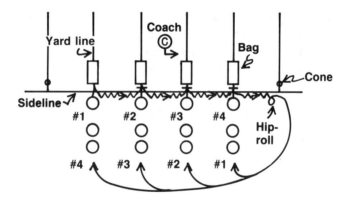

Diagram 11.4 In the Starts Drill, the coach points to the defender's right. The four-down strike a blow, shuffle to their right while shivering the end of the bags, hip roll, and then serpentine back to another bag.

"Five-Yard Shuffle-Run" Drill: Linebackers and Defensive Linemen

This lateral movement drill is used most often by the linebackers. It is also performed just outside of the field, utilizing the sideline and yard lines.

To set up the Five-Yard Shuffle-Run Drill, align the players outside the playing field single-file facing their coach, who is standing on the field. The first player should be just outside of the sideline in a two-point (linebacker) or a three-point (lineman) stance. As soon as he leaves to perform the drill, the next defender fills his spot.

Step 1. At the coach's movement, players slide laterally (shuffling and not crossing their feet), using perfect form—low, feet wide, shoulders parallel to the line, elbows inside with arms pumping.

Step 2. As they cross the next yard line (five yards), they open up and run laterally as fast as they can, again maintaining perfect form—shoulders low and parallel to the line of scrimmage.

Step 3. As they quickly reach the next yard line (five yards away), they resume their shuffling-sliding action. They continue to alternate their lateral movement between running and shuffling as they move down the side-line. This drill may be anywhere from twenty to fifty yards. After completing the drill, the players run back to the end of the line and do the same drill in the opposite direction. Diagram 11.5 illustrates the drill design.

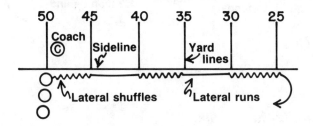

Diagram 11.5 The Five-Yard Shuffle-Run Drill.

"Shadow Shuffle-Run" Drill: Linebackers and Defensive Linemen

The next step in these progressive drills is to add a ball carrier to the shuffle-run. The linebackers (or defensive linemen) do not tackle the ball carrier, but practice maintaining a good half-a-man position behind the ball carrier as he alternates between shuffling and lateral runs.

To set up, align players in two single-file lines facing each other on the sideline: one line inside the field, the other outside.

Step 1. The player on the inside of the field assumes the role of the ball carrier and starts laterally down the sideline, alternating between a walk and a full sprint every five yards or so. He does not have to change his speed every five yards, but should attempt to alter it to "catch" the defender overpursuing, which is what the drill is trying to prevent.

Step 2. The defender, who is awaiting the designated ball carrier's initial movement from a good two-point (or lineman's three-point) stance, attempts to stay in an inside-out position by shuffling when the ball carrier is walking and running when the ball carrier runs. All of the defensive player's action must be performed, again, with perfect form.

Step 3. When the two participants come to the end of the run, the ball carrier crosses over the sideline and proceeds to the end of the defender's line. The defender crosses the line underneath the ball carrier and goes to the end of the ball carrier's line. Diagram 11.6 illustrates the drill's design.

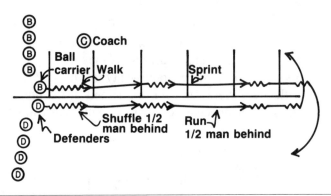

Diagram 11.6 The Shadow Shuffle-Run Drill.

"Bag Shuffle-Run" Drill:
Linebackers and Defensive Linemen

This drill is primarily for the front-eight, but because it appears to have great carry-over value, the secondary often use it as well. While being a practical strength and endurance conditioner, it also goes a long way in developing foot movement, coordination, balance, and the ability to use peripheral vision. This drill helps the defender go over or around obstacles (bodies) while pursuing the ball carrier as fast as possible.

The best setup for this drill uses seven large bags (but it still is a good drill if fewer are available). Again, using the sideline (or any lined area), lay seven large bags on their sides perpendicular to the sideline, with half the bag on the inside of the field and half outside. The two widest bags are ten yards apart, with the five remaining bags between them, separated by two or three feet. The players align single-file outside the field, and the coach positions himself on the field adjacent to the middle of the bags.

Step 1. The first player up starts the drill by shuffling back from his starting spot on the sideline, around the prone bag, and back to the sideline.

Step 2. As he reaches the sideline he immediately begins shuffling laterally (with perfect form) toward the five prone bags. (As soon as the first player moves around the first bag and reaches the sideline, the next player begins.) The player shuffles over the five inside bags, then upon reaching the last bag retreats around behind the bag and moves back up to the sideline.

Step 3.   As the player moves back up to the sideline after going around the last bag, he sprints with lateral running form for at least ten yards before circling back to repeat the drill. When the players circle back for the next drill repetition they align inside the field of play so that they do the drill to their left the next time around. The coach, of course, would then align outside the field of play. Diagram 11.7 illustrates the drill.

Some good coaching points for the Bag Shuffle-Run Drill are these:

- When players are shuffling over the bags, they should look straight ahead at the coach, seeing the bags in their peripheral vision.
- They should touch the bags with their hands as they go over them; in between bags they should pump their arms.
- They should never cross their feet, but step over the bags with the near foot first, staying low with their shoulders parallel to the line.

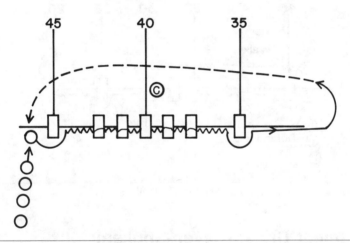

Diagram 11.7   The Bag Shuffle-Run Drill.

"Shadow-Bag Shuffle-Run" Drill: Linebackers and Defensive Linemen

This final drill in the series uses both the bags and a ball carrier to develop the defender's ability to move laterally and stay in a good position on the runner.

Set up this drill with the same bag arrangement as the previous drill, except use a twenty-yard boundary rather than the shorter ten-yard space. As they did in the Shadow Shuffle-Run Drill, the players designated as the ball carriers align single-file on the inside of the field, while the defenders align outside of the field facing the ball carriers.

Step 1.   The ball carrier initiates the drill by alternating between a walk and a sprint as he moves laterally, adjacent to the bags.

Step 2.   The defender now puts the skills learned in the Shadow Shuffle-Run Drill and the Bag Shuffle-Run Drill together. He has to work hard to stay in a good inside-out position on the ball carrier as he goes around or over the bags.

Step 3.   After passing the last bag, the ball carrier goes another five yards or so (a cone can be placed to mark the desired distance) before attempting to cross the line. The defender moves forward and makes a "form" tackle on the ball carrier. The two players will then move to the rear of the drill lines, opposite the ones in which they started. Diagram 11.8 illustrates this drill.

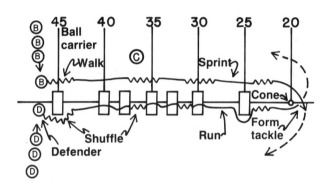

Diagram 11.8   The Shadow-Bag Shuffle-Run Drill.

Movement Drills: (Seven-Spokes)

While the front-eight are working primarily on their lateral movement, the secondary work on their backward action. The linebackers are considered part of the secondary when covering against the pass and thus must also work on their backward motion. Since the linebackers use the backward shuffle technique and the defensive backs do not, there are special drills just for linebackers.

"Backward-Shuffle Straight-Line" Drill: Linebackers

Using the junction of the yard lines and sideline, align four linebackers five yards apart on their respective yard line. Their initial position will be about five yards inside the sideline, facing the coach (positioned just outside the sideline) in a good two-point linebacker's stance. The remaining players wait in lines of four behind the coach.

Step 1.   When the coach raises the ball over his head, the linebackers shuffle straight back on their respective line, using perfect form.

Step 2.   After the linebackers have retreated about five yards, the coach points the ball to either side, and the linebackers execute the straight-line technique (described under the secondary's basic ART section), opening up and running at a 45° angle until they reach the next yard line.

Step 3.   As the linebackers reach the next yard line (five yards), they begin retreating, using the backward shuffle, down the yard line. They continue until the coach points the ball in the other direction, when they repeat their previous action, opening up at a 45° angle and running to the next yard line.

This action continues until the linebackers have retreated thirty or forty yards. When they are shuffling backward on a yard line, the coach can point the ball in either direction (he may repeat one direction several times). Remember, when the linebackers run laterally backward and reach the next line over (to their left or right), they should automatically start shuffling backward (without the coach signaling them to do so).

This drill can have many additions to its main scheme. For example, a ball may be thrown for the linebackers to intercept; the coach can move the ball to his stomach to signal a run, in which case the linebackers would

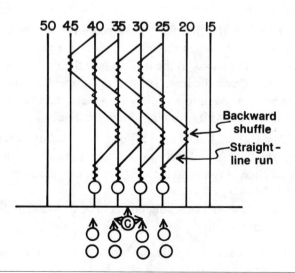

Diagram 11.9   The Backward-Shuffle Straight-Line Drill.

quickly stop and move forward; the ball could be pitched out to a ball carrier that the linebackers would pursue to with the proper pursuit angles. Diagram 11.9 illustrates the Backward-Shuffle Straight-Line Drill.

"Straight-Line" Drill: Defensive Backs

This is the most basic drill to teach backward running movement and is normally used two or three times a week. On Mondays this may be coupled with the Systematic Stance Drill.

The Straight-Line Drill is done many times with just one line of players. Our example shows the setup with all three defensive backs working together. Using the yard lines, the players position themselves five yards apart and about eight yards in from the sideline, facing the coach (who is outside of the sideline). The remaining players are in lines behind the coach, waiting their turns. The instant the three defensive backs in the drill begin retreating, the next set of three hustles out to fill the vacant spots.

Step 1.   The defensive backs await the coach's signal from perfect two-point stances; the outside two defenders face at a 45° angle to the outside, and the middle defensive back can face at a 45° angle in either direction. All three have their eyes and head pointed at the coach.

Step 2.   The coach raises the ball to one side, imitating a pass play, and the defenders retreat down their respective lines with their chests pointing to the side of the ball. (The coach pointing the ball to the right or left represents a quarterback who is looking in that direction to throw a pass; consequently, the secondary defenders use proper technique and point their chests in the same direction).

Step 3.   As soon as the first three have started down the line, another three take their places. When the coach moves the ball in the opposite direction, it signals to all six in the drill to face their chests in that direction as they retreat down the line. The original three defensive backs will have to pivot on their back foot as they turn their chest and shoulders in the opposite direction while running down the line.

Step 4.   This drill continues until all of the secondary defenders have moved across the field (about forty yards); they can either await the coach on the other sideline or return to their original spots. Diagram 11.10 illustrates this drill.

These are some essential coaching points to be included in the direction of the Straight-Line Drill:

- The defensive backs use only the straight-line line technique; they should never shuffle backward.

- The players never take their eyes off of the ball. Turning the head around and away from the ball when pivoting in the opposite direction is a big no-no!
- Players attempt to stay on the yard line as they are retreating.
- Players move only as fast as they are able while maintaining perfect form.
- This is a disciplined, repeating drill, in which the waiting players instantly fill the vacant spots, ready to go when the coach moves the ball to the other side.
- Defensive backs are taught to make calls and to talk to the other players. In all of the secondary drills, the three-deep yell "pass" when the quarterback (or linemen) signal pass; "ball" when the ball is released; "oskie" when they are in a position to intercept the ball; and "stick" when the ball carrier has passed the line of scrimmage and the play is definitely a run.
- Many additions and "wrinkles" may be added to this drill as you progress to teaching related skills.

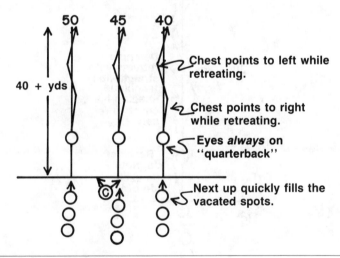

Diagram 11.10   The Straight-Line Drill.

"Straight-Line Chase" Drill: Defensive Backs

One of the best movement drills from the Straight-Line Drill is derived by adding a receiver to force the defender to use his straight-line skills under pressure.

Set up by positioning one defender on a yard line about eight yards from the sideline where the receiver is aligned. The coach is positioned off of the field, about five yards inside the receiver. The remaining players wait their turns behind the receiver.

Step 1.   The receiver sprints forward on the coach's signal, shading one side of the line or the other (he runs to a distance about two yards outside [or inside] the yard line). The defender reacts by retreating back with his chest pointed to the side of the receiver's path.

Step 2.   The receiver aims for a distance about two yards on the other side of the line as he sprints full speed ahead. The defensive back has to react by pivoting on his back foot and turning his chest in the receiver's new direction, while continuing to retreat and stay ahead of the receiver.

Step 3.   This action of the receiver crossing over the line and the defender shading his chest to the side of the receiver continues halfway across the field, or until the receiver passes up the defender. Diagram 11.11 illustrates the drill.

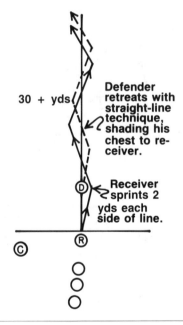

Diagram 11.11   The Straight-Line Chase Drill.

The Straight-Line Chase Drill has some points to be emphasized:

* The receiver's objective is to run the defender down before he gets halfway across the field (thirty yards or so) by getting the defender off-balance when pivoting from one direction to the other.

- You want the receiver to cross over to the other side of the line every five to seven yards to force the defender to use his straight-line pivoting technique.
- While running backward, pivoting, and staying ahead of the receiver, the defender is always looking at the coach (quarterback) and seeing the receiver in his peripheral vision.
- This is an excellent drill to reveal the skill levels of your defensive back personnel. The better they are, the closer they are able to line up from the receiver without being run down or forced off balance.
- Again, additions may be made to this drill to incorporate other skills and situations.

Defensive Adjustments

The extent of the effect that coaching can have on the final score of a game is always a good topic for debate among coaches. Many feel that the sport of football is one of the most "coachable" sports. One undisputed belief is that well-thought-out game plans have a definite positive effect on the final outcome. You might not have all the "stallions in your stables," but if you make the most of all the other aspects of coaching, including a sound and reasonable defensive game plan, you can usually survive.

Game-to-game adjustments are, of course, very important to any defense's success. With a multiple alignment defense, these adjustments are absolutely vital. A major reason for using a multiple defense is to create alignment advantages for your defenders, as well as to upset and confuse the offensive blocking schemes. These defensive adjustments must also be designed to take away from what the offense does best. If you can accomplish these objectives by defensive design alone, you have gone a long way in making up for any lack of physical talent your team may have versus an opponent. These are known as "guerrilla warfare" tactics, used when the enemy has too much firepower.

Because of the importance of the alignment variations to defensive success, it is essential that the players become familiar with each week's adjustments as early in the week as possible. If the adjustments mean that they will be playing from a different alignment much of the time, then they need as much practice time as possible to get comfortable with the new assignment. If the adjustment directs them to use a less used technique more often, they need more time to work on that technique. The defense's ability to recognize offensive alignments and to adjust to them properly also takes extra time and effort.

"Walk-and-Talk Adjustment Session" Drill: Entire Defense

A written and verbal scouting report should precede Monday's Walk-and-Talk. Players' understanding and retention of the various adjustments is greatly improved if you have explained beforehand the whys and why nots. Also, with prior information concerning the opponent's offense and the defense's plan, the adjustment practice drill goes a lot faster.

The adjustment session is very basic. It is not designed to present every feature of the upcoming opponent's offensive attack; rather, only the bread-and-butter formations, plays, and opponent's offensive strengths are reviewed. Any unique or exceptional attributes or deficiencies are also brought forth. The objective of this session is to help the defensive players form a mental picture of how the defense will stop their opponent's basic attack. Doing this on the first day of preparation for the upcoming foe gives the players adequate time to prepare both physically and mentally. Understanding early in the week how they are going to defeat their opponents promotes a positive and confident week's practice.

"Team Pursuit" Drill: Entire Defense

The Team Pursuit Drill needs to be well organized. It would probably be wise to explain the drill in a team meeting prior to its initiation. If thoroughly understood by the players, the drill works very smoothly; if not, it may look like a "Chinese fire drill." Because of the drill's significance, it is well worth the time needed to organize it properly. You may find that you like this drill as both a conditioner and a skill developer and choose to use it two or three days a week.

To set up, place five large bags, representing offensive linemen, on their sides three to four feet apart on the fifty-yard line. Behind the bags you will use extra players to assume the positions of quarterback, fullback, and two slotbacks, aligned just outside the widest bag on each side of the ball. Two wide receivers will also be used, split seventeen yards from the ball on each side. The defense will line up on the opposite side of the bags in their respective defensive positions. Various defensive sets may be used (especially those you expect to use against the upcoming opponent), but normally the defense practices this drill from the 44 Omaha defensive set. The coach will place himself behind the defensive safety, in a position to signal the desired offensive action to the five offensive players, without the defensive people's knowledge. The coach can signal the offensive people to run any one of five basic plays, but the first play—the pitch-out—is by far the most important and frequently run. The remaining four plays are used primarily to keep the defense "honest."

The coach uses simple hand signals to give the offense their plays. The plays, which can be run to either side, are as follows:

- Pitch-Out
- Inside Counter
- Reverse
- Long Pass
- Short Pass

Step 1.   The coach signals the play to the offense. Only the offensive players directly related to the play take part in the action. I will use the pitch-out as an example: The quarterback receives the ball on a center's snap, pivots, and pitches the ball to the fullback, who sprints around the end at full speed toward the end zone. He never stops, dodges, or changes direction as he heads toward the end zone.

Step 2.   The defensive players react to the play by moving to the ball carrier (or ball) using the shortest possible approach (referred to as the proper pursuit angle, or *tracks*). The four-down (defensive linemen) first shiver the ends of the bags that they are aligned over before getting into their pursuit angles to the runner.

Step 3.   The defenders pursue full speed in their proper tracks until they reach the runner. When they have gotten close enough to the runner to tag him (you can require them to tag the ball carrier but they may disrupt his progress), they stop, drop to their bellies and do one push-up. They then quickly get to their feet and sprint back to where the defensive huddle will form for the next play.

Step 4.   When they get back to the huddle area they should run in place, awaiting the arrival of the entire defense.

Step 5.   When a pass play is called, the defensive reaction is a little different. The four defensive linemen first shiver the bags and rush the passer as he retreats, then stop and let him throw the pass before sprinting in that direction. If it is a short pass, they run to the spot where the ball was caught, do their "belly slammer," and sprint to the huddle for the next play. If it is a long pass, they sprint back in the direction of the pass to a depth of ten yards, hit their bellies, and sprint to the huddle as before.

The seven-spokes attempt to intercept the ball on all pass plays. If they succeed, the entire defensive unit sprints the length of the field and across their opponent's goal line. If the offensive receiver catches the long pass, the defensive backs as well as the linebackers pursue to a "tagging" position, even if they have to run all the way to the goal line. If a pass play results in an incompletion, all defenders sprint back to the huddle.

It is crucial to the success of the Team Pursuit Drill that the defenders do not impede the unhindered progress of the ball carrier to the end zone.

Diagrams 11.12 through 11.16 demonstrate the defense's reaction and pursuit angles to each of the five plays.

When you first teach the pursuit angles to the defenders on the pitch-out and the other two running plays, have them walk through their pursuit directions as the ball carrier walks with the ball. You can then increase to a half-speed jog before having them pursue at full speed. Also, the backside end, whose responsibility is to trail as deep as the deepest back, does not have to chase the runner all the way to the goal line. He should trail the play until he passes the line of scrimmage on the other side of the ball, where he will hit his belly and sprint back to the huddle.

Tuesday's Practice Drills: ("Big D")

Includes

- Contact skill drills
- Reads and reaction drills
- Group and team drills

Drill descriptions will be limited to a few that are especially significant to the defense's success.

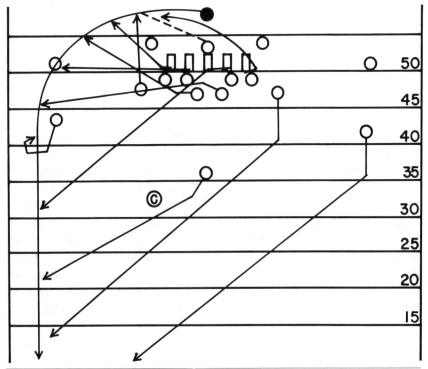

Diagram 11.12   Team Pursuit Drill—the Pitch-out.

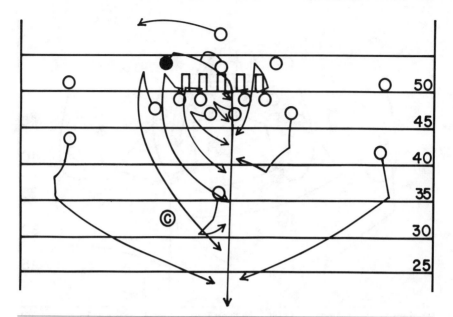

Diagram 11.13 Team Pursuit Drill—the Counter. The quarterback fakes the pitch-out and hands off to the slotback, who runs through the backside A gap.

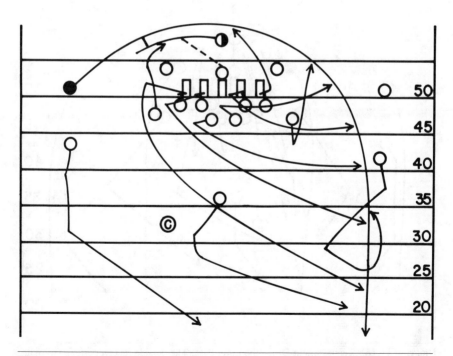

Diagram 11.14 Team Pursuit Drill—the Reverse. The quarterback pitches to the fullback who then hands off to the wide end reversing to the other side.

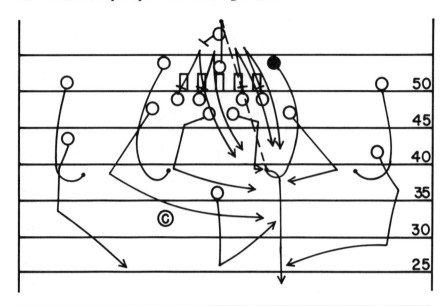

Diagram 11.15 Team Pursuit Drill—the Short Pass. All receivers run a twelve-yard curl pattern. Quarterback can throw to any one of them.

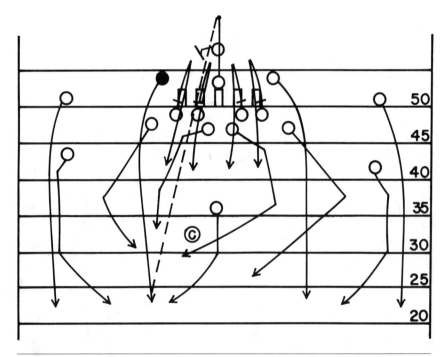

Diagram 11.16 Team Pursuit Drill—the Long Pass. The outside receivers run a Go route down the sidelines, and the two inside receivers run right down the hash marks.

"Hat" Drill: Defensive Linemen

The defensive linemen, especially the tackles, must work very hard to develop the skills necessary to gain the advantages that their alignment "shades" give them. The Hat Drill is a simple, fundamental drill that teaches the linemen how to read the offensive blocker's release direction and to quickly react with the proper technique.

Set up all of your defensive linemen by matching them in twos. Half of the players assume the role of the offensive blocker on one side of a line, and the other half work the drill. The offensive players position themselves about three yards apart in a normal three-point stance. The coach stands behind the defensive players to signal directions to the offensive people.

On the coach's snap count, the offensive players take one step in one of four directions (which could be determined by the coach). The four step-directions are listed here with the defender's reaction:

- Blocker steps inside: The defender shuffles a foot or two to his inside, simulating shutting-down the trap play, and responds as if he were delivering a blow to the blocker. (There is no contact in the initial Hat Drills, but they can be added later.)
- Blocker steps straight ahead: The defender steps forward and simulates delivering a defensive blow, or shiver.
- Blocker steps to outside: The defender shuffles a foot or two to his outside and simulates delivering a defensive blow and keeping the blocker off his outside leg.
- Blocker steps back and raises up: The defender moves forward, placing his forehand on the chest of the blocker, grabs the blocker's armpit area, and simulates using a defensive pass rush technique.

Points to emphasize to reap this drill's maximum benefit include having the players react as quickly as possible and with perfect form. As soon as the defenders read and react to the offensive blocker's movement, they quickly get right back into their stance and alignment position. The defenders may choose which alignment position to work from, and they can simulate delivering a blow using either the tripod or the flipper technique. This drill is often done without the coach's direction. Each pair works at its own pace, with the offensive man simulating the blocker's movements while the defender reacts. Diagrams 11.17a, b, c, and d illustrate the offensive blockers making the four basic moves, with the defenders' corresponding reactions.

Diagram 11.17a   In the Hat Drill, the blocker steps to the inside, and the defender shuffles inside and imitates a defensive blow.

Diagram 11.17b   The blocker steps straight ahead, and the defender steps up and imitates a defensive blow.

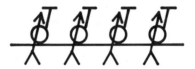

Diagram 11.17c   The blocker steps outside, and the defender shuffles outside, imitating a defensive blow.

Diagram 11.17d   The blocker steps back and raises up; the defender moves toward him and imitates a pass rush technique.

The Hat Drill is a fundamental base drill with many progressive versions. It starts as a noncontact, one-on-one drill and advances to a full contact drill with as many as seven offensive people against the four defensive linemen. The Hat Drill also is used quite often with the linebackers.

"Dodge" Drill: Defensive Linemen

This has proved to be one of our better contact drills to teach the defensive linemen to aggressively react to the offensive blocker's movement and to deliver a good solid defensive blow.

You can set up this drill one-on-one or with as many as four-on-four performing at one time. For the one-on-one drill, align two large bags about three yards apart with one end of each bag resting on a yard line. One player represents the offensive blocker and aligns in a three-point stance between the bags, just outside of the bag ends that are farthest away from the yard line. A large cone is placed seven yards directly behind the offensive blocker. The defensive man will align in a #2, #3, or #4 alignment over the blocker, between the bags.

Step 1.   The offensive blocker, on his own count, attempts to sprint past the defender (to either side), staying inside the bags. The defender reacts to the offensive lineman's lateral and forward movement by quickly moving toward the blocker in a position to deliver a defensive blow and deny the blocker's movement over the yard line. If the defender stops the offensive blocker and knocks him over the bags, he wins!

Step 2.   The blocker may choose to pass block. If he steps back and sets up, the defender must attempt to knock over the cone placed behind the blocker in four seconds to win the battle. Diagram 11.18 illustrates the drill setup.

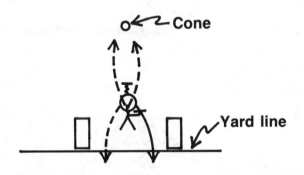

Diagram 11.18   The Dodge Drill.

"Three-on-Two" Drill: Defensive Tackles

There are various matchups that you can use to work the defensive line versus opponents' different blocking schemes. The defensive tackles will work from two-on-two, three-on-two, five-on-two, and seven-on-four with the entire defensive line. The Three-on-Two Drill is probably used most often to work just with the defensive tackles because it requires only a few players to provide the blocking schemes that are of primary concern to the defensive tackles. With three offensive blockers (with or without the use of one running back), you are able to run the off-tackle scoop block play and the inside trap. To work against an offensive tackle's double-team and fold block schemes, it is simple to have one of the offensive guards move over and align with the other guard as an offensive tackle. With this arrangement you work the one defensive tackle three-on-one. Diagrams 11.19a and b illustrate the defensive tackles working against two primary blocking schemes.

Place two large bags approximately five yards apart on a yard line to set up. Three offensive linemen align inside the bags at the bags' front edges. A running back can be added and aligned five yards behind the center. The coach positions himself behind the defensive tackles and signals the snap count and blocking schemes to the offensive group.

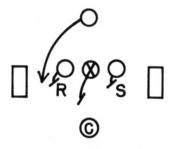

Diagram 11.19a   The Three-on-Two Drill against the off-tackle scoop or block play.

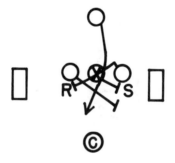

Diagram 11.19b   The Three-on-Two Drill against the inside trap play.

"Tight-Three" Drill: Inside Linebackers

One of two good inside linebacker drills, the Tight-Three Drill emphasizes protecting the inside area and reading the triangle.

Set up by aligning an offensive center and two guards with three-foot splits on a yard line, with one running back placed five yards behind the center. Two large bags are placed outside of each offensive guard. The

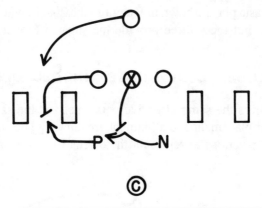

Diagram 11.20a The Tight-Three Drill against the off-tackle play.

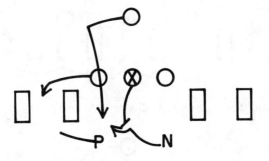

Diagram 11.20b The Tight-Three Drill against the cut-back play.

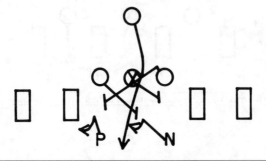

Diagram 11.20c The Tight-Three Drill against the inside trap play. Emphasize that the onside-inside linebacker should not come up inside the bags so far that he can't get to the outside. It is the defensive tackle's responsibility to shut down the inside trap running lane.

first bag is about one yard outside, and the second bag is two yards wider than the inside bag. The inside linebackers align as close to the offensive guards as they can while still being able to successfully react to the plays. The coach stands behind the linebacker and signals the snap count and one of three basic plays, shown in Diagrams 11.20a, b, and c. Other plays can be added, but these three provide the substance of the drill.

"Wide-Three" Drill: Inside Linebackers

This drill utilizes the same offensive personnel and the same four large bags, but their placement and alignment are altered. The bags are laid on a yard line in positions to represent the offensive guards and tight ends,

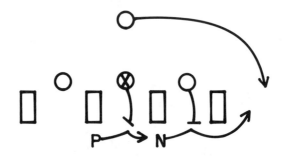

Diagram 11.21a The Wide-Three Drill against the sweep.

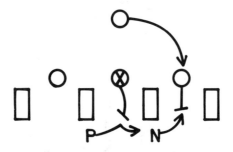

Diagram 11.21b The Wide-Three Drill against the off-tackle play.

Diagram 11.21c The Wide-Three Drill against the cut-back play.

about three yards apart. An offensive center aligns inside and in front of the two inside bags, and the offensive tackles align inside and in front of the outside bags. The linebackers align just behind the two inside bags that represent the offensive guards' positions. The coach again stands behind the linebackers and signals one of three plays to the offense. Diagrams 11.21a, b, and c illustrate the sweep, off-tackle, and cut-back plays.

"Four-on-Two Perimeter" Drill: Defensive Ends and Outside Linebackers

When the defensive ends and outside linebackers have attained sufficient skill in basic reads and defeating the block, they advance to the Four-on-Two Perimeter Drill. This drill, like most, can be supplemented with other personnel, plays, and alignments.

Set up by aligning a tailback, an onside halfback, a tight end, and a quarterback (who could be the coach) in a "power" alignment on a yard

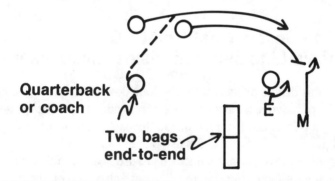

Diagram 11.22a The Four-on-Two Perimeter Drill against the sweep.

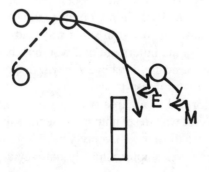

Diagram 11.22b The Four-on-Two Perimeter Drill against the off-tackle play.

line. Two large bags are placed end-to-end inside and in front of the defensive end's position. A defensive end aligns in a #3 position on the tight end, with the outside linebacker assuming his normal alignment. (This defensive alignment could be varied by having the outside linebacker and defensive end aligning in a Wide formation.) The three base plays run against the perimeter defenders are illustrated in Diagrams 11.22a, b, and c.

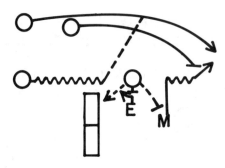

Diagram 11.22c   The Four-on-Two Perimeter Drill against the option play.

"Five-on-Seven West Point" Drill: Defensive Linemen and Inside Linebackers

Although this drill is primarily for the four-down and inside linebackers, a position for a defensive back to take part is added, and the outside linebackers can participate from the inside linebacker positions or the defensive end positions. So every defensive player can actually take part at one time or another. Five offensive linemen are used with a "full-house" backfield. Four additional offensive receivers are also used on the pass plays. The players that are not in the drill align outside the drill area and encourage those that are. This drill and its more basic counterpart, the Three-on-Three West Point Drill are, in my opinion, the best drills in football. Everyone on the team is involved in some way, either playing or cheering. You find out who the hitters are and who has that special "football instinct" and desire. Basically, I believe you will find out who really wants to play football and who doesn't.

This drill is performed in an area twenty yards wide and twenty-five yards long. The easiest way to set it up is to use the sideline as one boundary, use the yard lines to find the twenty-yard width, and then march off the length by putting cones approximately halfway across the field. Six large bags are laid across the sideline, three yards apart, in the middle of the side boundaries. The offense, five linemen and four backs, aligns outside of the field facing the sideline. Four receivers are placed outside the drill area. Two are positioned fifteen yards deep, just outside of the field. The other two are twenty-five yards deep on the outside corner of the field. The four-down defenders and the inside linebackers normally align in a Tight 44 set, but they may use any of the standard calls. The defensive back aligns about ten yards deep, in front of the offensive center (the defensive back can only tackle a ball carrier once he has gone ten yards or more). The coach positions himself behind the defensive back, where he can signal the snap count and play to the offense.

Six basic plays are used, with the coach signaling the information to the offense. The plays are these:

- Dive (halfback or fullback)
- Quick Pitch-out
- Cross-buck

- Belly Option
- Short Pass
- Long Pass

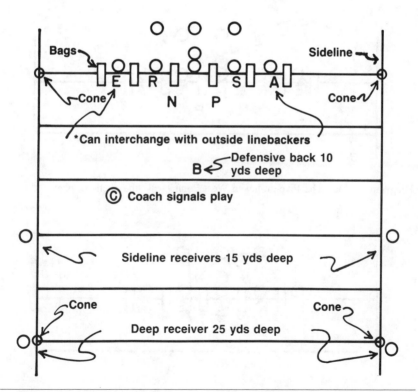

Diagram 11.23a   The Five-on-Seven West Point Drill setup.

All running plays are blocked straight ahead, and the pass plays are drop-back action with Man-to-Man blocking. Diagrams 11.23a through g demonstrate the drill layout and the six basic plays.

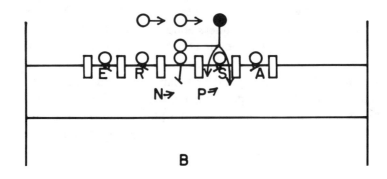

Diagram 11.23b　The Dive play, which could also be called the fullback dive.

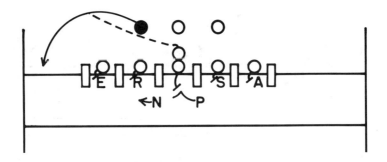

Diagram 11.23c　The Five-on-Seven West Point Drill—the pitch-out play.

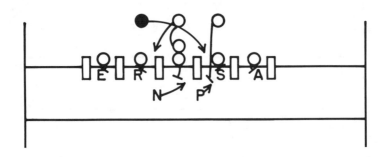

Diagram 11.23d　The Cross-buck play.

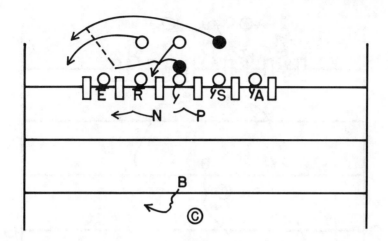

Diagram 11.23e The Belly Option.

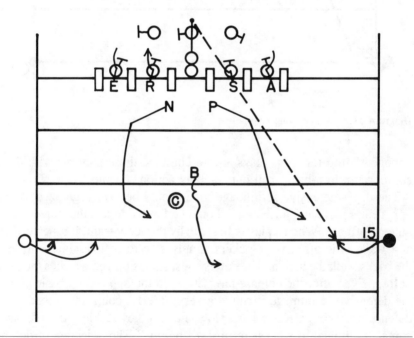

Diagram 11.23f The Five-on-Seven West Point Drill—the Short Pass.

Tuesday's three-deep secondary drills are technique- and coverage-related. Receivers are added to form one-on-one, three-on-two, and three-on-three drills. Each coverage technique is practiced in proportion to the amount of its use. The Omaha coverage is run most, followed by Buckeye and Kansas Man-to-Man. You want to run your coverages against the

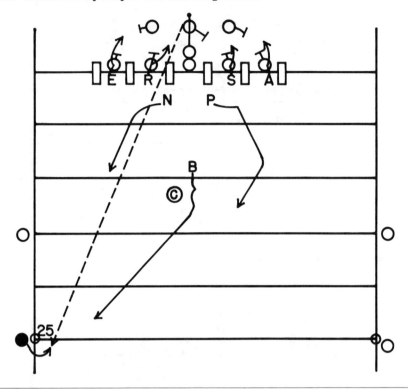

Diagram 11.23g The Long Pass.

opponent's top few pass plays and to combine those patterns with their appropriate drop-back, roll-out, or play action scheme.

Tuesday's defensive scrimmage time should be very organized. Your opponent's plays and formations should be limited to just the "bread-and-butter" offense. When a play is first run by the scout team, it is performed at a walk. The offensive blockers simply step to their assignment, and the backs walk the action. The defense just stands up and watches the play unfold. Even after the defense has witnessed the opponent's basic plays, the defensive scrimmage is run at a very orderly, controlled speed. The defense does not deliver a hard blow, nor do they tackle. All defensive contact is limited to what is termed a "bump." The objective of defensive scrimmages is for the players to gain a mental picture of the opponent's offense, while being able to visualize their proper reactions and pursuit angles. Full-speed contact can be brought into defensive scrimmages in "challenge" situations. The scout team may challenge the defense with four plays, etc. This is usually done at the end of the scrimmage period, for fun, in the goal line area.

Wednesday's Practice Drills:
("Polish")

Wednesday's practice is called "Polish," and for the defense it means just that! Your situation defenses (goal line, long yardage, short yardage) and the opponent's special formations and plays are reviewed. Defensive practice is confined mainly to large group and full team drills.

Thursday's Practice Drills:
("Hay-Day")

Thursday's practice, named "Hay-Day," wraps up the week's practice. For the defense it is question-and-answer and special-team time. An offensive group is aligned in the upcoming opponent's specific formations, with standard down and distance situations, and the defense is asked to make the correct adjustments. Every scrimmage situation should be covered so that both coaches and players know that they know what to do. The punt rush and return are reviewed, and the kickoff is given sufficient time to allow the players to leave the field believing that they will recover the first onside kick.

About the Author

With over 30 years of experience as a coach and player, Bill Siler knows the game of football. During his 18 years as head football coach, he was named Oregon State AA Coach of the Year once and League Coach of the Year six times. With a record of 113 wins, 60 losses, and 3 ties, he's led his teams to nine league championships and one Oregon State Championship. While attending Pierce Junior College in Woodland Hills, California, Bill was selected for the Junior College All-American Team; later he was a three-year letterman as quarterback/halfback at the University of Washington.

After receiving his BS degree from the University of Washington at Seattle, Bill went on to earn his MEd from Eastern Washington State University at Cheney. He has published two articles in *Scholastic Coach Magazine*, ''The GTS ''T'' Set,'' May, 1967, and ''Getting the Ball Back With the Kamikaze Kickoff,'' October, 1985. Currently, Bill teaches math and is an assistant coach at Grant High School in Portland, Oregon.